Advertising and Marketing to the New Majority

Gail Baker Woods
University of Missouri
School of Journalism

Wadsworth Publishing Company
I(T)P™ An International Thomson Publishing Company

Belmont • Albany • Bonn • Boston • Cincinnati • Detroit • London
Madrid • Melbourne • Mexico City • New York • Paris • San Francisco
Singapore • Tokyo • Toronto • Washington

Dedication: **To my mother, Ann C. Baker, for all that I am and all I ever hope to become.**

Advertising Editor: Todd R. Armstrong
Editorial Assistants: Joshua King and Laura Murray
Production Editors: Carol Dondrea and Robin Lockwood
Designer: Suzanne Montazer

Print Buyer: Randy Hurst
Permissions Editor: Robert Kauser
Copy Editor: Melissa Andrews
Cover Designer: Ross Carron
Compositor: Fog Press
Printer: Malloy Lithographing

For more information, contact Wadsworth Publishing Company.

Wadsworth Publishing Company
10 Davis Drive
Belmont, California 94002
USA

International Thomson Editores
Campos Eliseos 385, Piso 7
Col. Polanco
11560 México D.F. México

International Thomson Publishing Europe
Berkshire House 168–173
High Holborn
London, WC1V7AA
England

International Thomson Publishing GmbH
Königswinterer Strasse 418
53227 Bonn
Germany

Thomas Nelson Australia
102 Dodds Street
South Melbourne 3205
Victoria, Australia

International Thomson Publishing Asia
221 Henderson Road
#05–10 Henderson Building
Singapore 0315

Nelson Canada
1120 Birchmount Road
Scarborough, Ontario
Canada M1K 5G4

International Thomson Publishing Japan
Hirakawacho Kyowa Building, 3F
2-2-1 Hirakawacho
Chiyoda-ku, Tokyo 102
Japan

Library of Congress Cataloging-in-Publication Data

Woods, Gail Baker.
    Advertising and marketing to the new majority / Gail Baker Woods.
        p.   cm.
    Includes bibliographical references and index.
    ISBN 0-534-24192-1
    1. Advertising—United States. 2. Marketing—United States. 3. Minorities as consumers—United States. 4. Ethnic groups—United States. 5. Advertising—United States—Case studies. 6. Marketing—United States—Case studies. I. Title.
HF5813.U6W635   1995
658.8'348—dc20
                                                          94-27899

C O N T E N T S

PART I The Changing Marketplace

PART II **Case Studies**

P R E F A C E

The questions are all too familiar to advertisers. How do we best reach our audiences with timely and interesting information about the products and services we offer? What do consumers need and want to know about us? How do we break through the clutter of myriad advertising and marketing messages? What compels people to buy and to become loyal to a particular brand?

As we all know, the answers to these questions have never been simple. But in today's world of diverse consumers, evolving markets, and new media, solutions to these issues are more complicated than ever. Audiences have changed. Many are immigrants who have come to the United States seeking a better life. Others are indigenous to this country, but their race or ethnicity distinguishes them from the mainstream culture. All are just awakening to their buying power and consumer clout.

On the one hand, racial and ethnic minorities—African Americans, Hispanic Americans, Asian Americans, and Native Americans—have a number of things in common with each other. Their numbers are steadily growing, and they share a common thread with all other Americans—they consume products. Thus, it is important to understand how they respond to advertising messages and what they expect from marketers. On the other hand, ethnic minorities are unlike each other and different from the mainstream in the way in which they hear, view, and interpret advertising messages.

That is what this book is about and how it came to be written. The advertising community is grappling with the best way to provide information to emerging audiences. Educators are seeking ways to teach students to be persuasive communicators in a rapidly changing marketplace. This book addresses these issues by looking at successful and not-so-successful campaigns aimed at ethnic audiences.

Advertising and Marketing to the New Majority is a compilation of cases from ethnic and nonethnic advertising agencies in the forefront of the changing business environment. It discusses special efforts aimed at ethnic audiences and the challenges facing those who wish to penetrate this market. Specifically, it focuses on what has been learned about how to appeal to ethnic audiences.

The book is divided into two parts. Part I is an overview of the changing marketplace, including the evolution of ethnic advertising, ethnic consumer behavior, and the legal and social environment in which advertising and marketing operates. Part II presents 11 case studies. Each case begins with an overview of a company attempting to appeal to ethnic groups. This background sets the stage for the campaign. Following the company profile is a discussion of what the company wanted to accomplish, how it executed the campaign, and the results of the campaign. Instructors can assign cases to groups or individual students. They can also use this format to have students develop entirely new campaigns based on what is discussed and learned from the cases presented.

A special feature of the book is a section following each case called "View from the Top." In this section, we interview industry leaders, who share their insights, frustrations, and expertise. Each interview is preceded by a brief biography.

Discussion questions follow each chapter and case, and teachers can either use these or create their own.

The last chapter includes major lessons drawn from each case. These are based on what I learned. Readers can draw their own conclusions.

The book is aimed at upper-level college students enrolled in marketing, journalism, advertising, and mass communication courses. It is designed to stand alone as a text for a course in ethnic advertising, or to be used as a supplement in a survey course on advertising and/or marketing. Some professors find it difficult to incorporate this topic into the basic goals of their courses because the subject is often viewed as specialized information rather than as an integral part of advertising and marketing. However, the text is intended for all students of advertising or marketing because it highlights, discusses, and analyzes cases from the perspective of what is effective advertising—no matter what the audience or product.

The text approaches advertising and marketing to the new majority from a practical perspective. Students are privy to the plans, objectives, and executions of campaigns. They are treated as insiders who can bring their expertise to the cases. They have a chance to critique the work of professionals and decide how they might have done it better.

I wrote this book because, as a teacher, I wanted my students to understand the importance of target marketing. I could find no better way to teach marketing segmentation than to discuss it in terms of new and unique audiences. Looking at advertising from the standpoint of ethnic audiences offers a chance to teach simultaneously segmentation, racial sensitivity, good copywriting technique, research, strategy, management, psychology, and consumer behavior.

It's no secret that the government projects a continuous increase in minority populations. These growth factors, combined with declines in advertising budgets, the popularity of specialized media, and always present economic uncertainty, portend a move toward even more efficient and, it is hoped, effective advertising programs. This text will help prepare students for what they will face as professionals.

For the purposes of this text, markets are defined in terms of ethnic groups. Subgroups of the majority population such as Italians, Poles, Jews, Greeks, and others are not dealt with. A number of terms are used to describe these ethnic groups. Because there is no designation on which all members of the audience agree, several names are used interchangeably. For example, African Americans are sometimes referred to as blacks or black Americans; Hispanic Americans are, in some cases, called Latino. The terms used were gathered from the advertising agencies and reflect the words they use to describe their audiences.

I found the topic of advertising and marketing to the new majority to be timely and, just as important, fun. This book takes a serious look at the ad game without taking advertising too seriously.

➤ Acknowledgments

Many people helped with this project. My first thanks to God, through whom all is possible. A special thanks to my colleagues Dr. Lee Wilkins, for the title, and Dr. Betty Winfield, who urged me to set a research agenda around a topic I enjoyed. I am grateful to the advertising executives who opened their offices to me, including Tom Burrell, Sam Chisholm, Vince Cullers, Adriane Gaines, Valerie Graves, Joseph Lam, Byron Lewis, Marta Miyares, J. Melvin Muse, Carlos Rossi, and Dana Yamagata. I would also like to thank the following reviewers for their comments: Linda J. Shipley, University of Nebraska, Lincoln; Marilyn Kern-Foxworth, Texas A&M University; Jim Pokrywczynski, Marquette University; Peggy J. Kreshel, University of Georgia; and Esther Thorson, University of Wisconsin. It would have been impossible to complete this book without the help of my two research assistants, Nileeni Meegama and Lillie Fears, and my administrative assistant, Kathy Sharp. Thank you, too, to Todd Armstrong, who believed in the project when others didn't.

I would also like to acknowledge the support of my family and friends. Thanks to my husband Bob, for his patience and affection, and my sister Linda, who has been my role model since the beginning. Thanks to my father John and my sister Jackie and my mother-in-law Roslyn, for their continued encouragement. I am eternally grateful to my best friend, Deirdre Allen, who has been a part of everything I've ever done. And last, but most importantly, to my daughter, Ryann Erika, who waited exactly one day after I completed this manuscript to be born.

The
Changing
Marketplace

Introduction to Ethnic Advertising and Marketing

"Target marketing is a redundant term. All effective marketing is targeted. Ethnic advertising has always been aimed at specific audiences and therefore, is at the forefront of what we call target marketing."

—Tom Burrell

In this introduction to ethnic advertising and marketing, the intriguing and diverse nature of these emerging markets is revealed. This chapter discusses the influence of ethnic culture on general market advertising and reviews recent developments and new trends. The importance of subcultures, ethnic images, and portrayals in advertising is emphasized, as is the role of ethnic advertising agencies.

On finishing this chapter you should be able to do the following:

1. Define what distinguishes the ethnic market from the general market
2. Identify the common threads between the two markets
3. Explain the viability of the ethnic market
4. Describe why and how ethnic marketing leads the way for the study of marketing segmentation

Why Study Ethnic Marketing?

There are several compelling reasons to study ethnic marketing. First and most obvious is the growth in spending power of the ethnic markets in America. By the year 2000, one in two, or 50 percent of all elementary school children in America, will be ethnic minorities.[1] Nearly half (44 percent) of all U.S. residents under the age of 20 will also be nonwhite.[2] Marketers will not be able to survive unless they can tap this major economic force.

A second reason to study ethnic marketing is because old markets for products change, die out, or shift priorities. Again, product survival is contingent on the marketers' ability to uncover new places to sell products.

Third, economic instability has created a trend toward careful segmentation of the target audience as a means of avoiding waste and optimizing message exposure and acceptance. Corporate profits began to plummet in the early 1990s, and with the fall in profits came a decrease in advertising spending. In 1991, the Television Bureau of Advertising reported that network ad spending fell more than 7 percent over 1990 figures. Newspaper ad spending dropped by the same amount during the same period, according to the Newspaper Advertising Bureau, and magazine ad revenues dropped 5 percent.[3] It is doubtful that advertising will ever experience the type of boom it enjoyed in the 1970s and 1980s, when spending grew faster than the overall U.S. economy.[4]

There are myriad reasons for the precipitous declines in advertising spending. Consumers are exposed to more messages than they can absorb. The average adult consumer is bombarded with at least 500 advertising and marketing messages daily according to some experts.[5] Others estimate the number to be as high as 3,000 messages.[6] The result is less recall of messages. According to a report from Video Story Board Tests, a market researcher, in 1986 viewer retention of ads they had seen in the previous month was 64 percent. Four years later, only 48 percent retained the message.[7]

Technology has also influenced the manner in which products are sold. Computerized market research can provide detailed information about target audiences; for example, names and addresses can be matched with consumer habits.

Direct marketing, once known as junk mail, has grown in scope and often competes head on with advertising. Its main benefit is that it is more targeted than advertising.

A housing developer in Chesterfield, Missouri, sends videotapes to prospective buyers. Cadillac offered a videotape presentation by mail to 170,000 potential owners of its cars. The Marriott Corporation gives prospective time-share condo buyers a videotape to take home after they have visited the properties. It features pictures of families enjoying the benefits of vacationing with Marriott. Spiegel teamed with *Ebony* magazine to introduce a catalog expressly for black women. *E-Style* features stylish clothing, bold colors, and special sizing designed for the body shapes and lifestyles of African American females. Spiegel placed inserts in its regular catalogs and offered a special 800 number on its billing statements inviting black women to order *E-Style*.

New media outlets, cable television, and specialty magazines all tend to cut the target market into narrower and more clearly delineated slices.

As the majority population declines and the ethnic population increases, there will be more opportunity for these targeted messages to reach the households of African Americans, Hispanic Americans, Asian Americans, and Native Americans. How will these markets react to direct mail pieces that feature only Caucasians or show ethnic people in unlikely and unrealistic situations? The likely response will be, "They're obviously not marketing to me." Affluent ethnic consumers will simply have the choice to spend their money elsewhere.

Ethnic marketing is actually a trend-setting technique from which the basic principles of segmentation can be learned and applied. The nuances and diversity of the ethnic market provide a platform for the study of all marketing. Marketers who are able to dissect and penetrate complex and diverse ethnic markets can segment markets along urban or rural lines, national and international audiences, youth and senior audiences, or any other markets that might emerge in the future.

⟩ The Growth of Ethnic Subcultures

Cultural homogeneity does not exist, nor has it ever existed in the United States. Ethnicity has always been a part of the nation's social character. For the most part, subcultures have lived in harmony with the mainstream. Berkman and Gilson define subculture as "any cultural patterning that preserves important features of the dominant society but provides values and life styles of its own."[8] Chicago, for example, is known as a city of ethnic neighborhoods and a place where cultural heritage is celebrated. There are Polish communities,

Irish Catholic neighborhoods, and Greek enclaves, to name a few. Members of these groups often live near each other, worship together, enjoy the same standard of living, and share similar values.

The great migration of African Americans from the South after World War II, an increase in immigrants from Mexico and Puerto Rico, and a steady stream of Asian newcomers have changed the face and color of ethnic groups in the United States. Although they are easily distinguishable from the mainstream, that is, Caucasian ethnic groups, they, too, view themselves as Americans.

For ethnic minority groups, like other segments of the society, subcultures play an important role. Through membership in a subculture, minorities are able to find identity, cohesiveness, and unity. Subcultural behavior is a means through which heritage and pride can be openly communicated. Certain styles of dress, sometimes considered unacceptable to mainstream society, can be worn within the subculture without fear of rejection. The same can be said for hairstyles, use of language, and celebrations of events. For example, in New York's Chinatown, it is preferable to speak Chinese and read publications written in Chinese. In Atlanta, African shops and boutiques market colorful garb from Nigeria, Ghana, and a host of other nations. In Chicago, Puerto Ricans celebrate their heritage with a major parade that blocks the downtown streets for one day each year.

In each of these cases, and in many more similar examples, subculture participation has become a means of protecting and preserving what is unique and distinct about specific groups of people. While most members of these communities subscribe to America's "melting pot" theory, they are not interested in becoming indistinguishable ingredients of a bland national stew.

The lesson for marketers is that it is possible to reach minority ethnic consumers on two levels, as they exist in two separate worlds. Because they are Americans, messages of patriotism, nationalism, and participation can be effective, but their strong adherence to tradition and heritage means that messages with cultural appeal also have merit.

Ethnic Audiences and the Marketing Mix

All products and services have a life cycle. From the time a product idea is generated to the day when the marketer decides it is no longer viable, efforts are focused on pushing the product through the distribution channel. Most often, the strategy used to achieve the overriding goal of product success includes the marketing mix, which consists of the four P's (product, price, promotion, and place).

Not all people respond the same to the marketing mix, and ethnic groups are no exception. In developing a product for ethnic groups, marketers must ask if the good or service they have in mind will fulfill some consumer need. When Johnson Products created the Afro-Sheen hair products line in the late 1960s, it was responding to the black community's heightened awareness of its African heritage. The Afro hairstyle was a way of outwardly expressing one's "blackness." Good grooming did not take a back seat to cultural heritage for Afro-Americans at the time, so a product was needed that would allow for both. Afro-Sheen ads used African language and created a campaign around the phrase "Wantu Wanzuri," which was the Swahili translation for "beautiful people."

Price, too, plays an important role with ethnic consumers. Although some would assume that members of ethnic groups tend to pay less for products and services, research indicates that, in many cases, they are willing and able to pay more. The marketing of Remy Martin XO cognac to Asian Americans is one example of this. At over $100 a bottle, this drink is out of the price range for many consumers. However, the company established a campaign to associate the expensive brand with special occasions, or times when price is no object.

Place also plays a critical role in marketing products to ethnic audiences. That is, the availability of the product at the places where they shop is an important consideration. For example, African Americans are frequent purchasers of fast food, and they are also highly concentrated in urban areas. Marketers like McDonald's and KFC (formerly Kentucky Fried Chicken) may have a number of restaurants in a densely populated urban area, and often within walking distance of consumers. Suburban customers are likely to drive a short distance to get to their local fast-food establishment.

Members of the Hispanic community tend to be impressed with promotions. They want a company to demonstrate its interest in them and their families. According to Patricia V. Asip, manager of corporate special segment marketing at J. C. Penney, "Research shows clearly that Hispanic consumers buy from companies that are sensitive to their language needs and become involved with Hispanic community events."[9] In response to this, J. C. Penney sponsored major promotional campaigns around five Hispanic holidays, including Three Kings Day, Cinco de Mayo, Puerto Rican Day, Dies y Seis (Mexican Independence Day), and Columbus Day.[10]

Traditional channels of marketing products may be effective in reaching ethnic audiences, but specialized vehicles can prove to be even more effective. How a product is conceived, how it is positioned, where it can be purchased, and what it costs are all significant considerations for ethnic audiences, and thus important issues for product marketers trying to reach them.

What Ethnic Cultures Contribute to Mainstream Advertising

Once called "jungle music" and the "ghetto sound," the distinctive chords of African American music are now a ubiquitous staple in television advertising. The soulful melodies of Ray Charles and the "Uh-Huh" girls have been the cornerstone of Diet Pepsi's 1990s campaign. Kid 'N Play, a popular rap duo, mixed music and dance in promoting Sprite. Aretha Franklin, in an almost sacrilegious gospel rendition of "Deliver Me," urged Pizza Hut fans to pick up the phone. C & C Music Factory converted their popular hit song "Everybody Dance Now" into a Coke commercial. The smooth sounds of Stevie Wonder added sentimentality to Kodak cameras, who used Bill Cosby as its primary spokesperson. And rap artist Hammer lost all of his "soul" until he was given a "proper" can of Pepsi. Before Hammer, Michael Jackson was paid an estimated $6 million to sing for Pepsi. In one of its general market campaigns, Burger King used a flaming piano being played by a black musician to demonstrate just how hot flame-broiled burgers could get.

Even when African Americans are not featured in the visuals of ads, their music can be heard. Aretha Franklin's "Natural Woman" was used to enhance the image of Chic jeans. The cooking spray Pam even made an effort (though mangled) to create a rap song about vegetable oil in aerosol form. "Pam, Pam, Pa Pam . . . Have you thought about Pam, butter flavor?" was the opening line of the commercial.

From black dance and music to black "lingo," advertising has based some of its most successful campaigns on black culture and/or black personalities. Why is African American music so readily accepted by the advertising industry to promote products? Byron Lewis, president and chief executive officer (CEO) of UniWorld, attributed this trend to the mainstream's interest in and curiosity about black culture. "Black people have traditionally set trends in fashion, style, language, and particularly, entertainment," Lewis said. "Black culture is perceived to be more cutting edge. What appeals to young blacks often appeals to young whites. Blacks set the market trends in the 1980s."[11]

With this in mind, advertisers use black cultural images to impart a variety of themes and to appeal to a wider audience. A jeans manufacturer traveled to a New York City street corner to give its product an urban identity. A detergent maker went to a black church to sing the praises of its cleaning agents. Basketball great Michael Jordan was teamed with movie director Spike Lee in an ad designed to reach both black and white audiences. Later, Jordan was paired with contemporary Larry Byrd.

The popularity of African American musical culture in commercial advertising is rivaled only by the industry's use of black athletes. Michael Jordan eats Wheaties, wears Hanes underwear, drinks Coke and Gatorade (not together, it is hoped), and eats at McDonald's. In Chicago, following the 1991 Bulls championship season, McDonald's created the McJordan, a burger covered in barbeque sauce—the way Michael is said to prefer them. Young people of all ages would like to "be like Mike."

Heavyweight boxer Evander Holyfield would rather eat in Burger King. Magic Johnson plays his own video games, and retired heavyweight boxer George Foreman likes chicken from KFC and has his car muffler repaired at Midas.

According to the London International Advertising Awards Committee, "Bo Knows" plenty. They applauded the Nike "Just Do It" campaign featuring Bo Jackson, by presenting it with their top honors for 1991.[12]

Basketball superstar Shaquille O'Neal's image has been used to sell athletic shoes, Pepsi, sports drinks, and clothing. In fact, "Shaq's" 7-foot 3-inch shadow looms so large it even spread to his father. The elder O'Neal, an army officer, has his own television commercial in which he smashes a glass telephone booth, emulating the behavior of his son, who is known for breaking the glass on basketball backboards.

The phenomenon of using African American athletes is not new. In the 1950s, Jackie Robinson, the first black major league baseball player, was used in cigarette advertising aimed at blacks. A memorable campaign for Hertz rental cars involved football great O. J. Simpson flying through an airport. (If he could fly, why was he there?)

In the 1970s, football player Rosie Greer used Bounty paper towels. Retired football player Fred "the Hammer" Williamson was used to promote the attributes of malt liquor (a product often aimed at African Americans), and former Pittsburgh Steeler "Mean" Joe Green was featured in a classic Coca-Cola ad.

While some applaud the use of black athletes to promote products, such images are not without critics. Some complain that the use of black athletes tends to promote stereotypes of the black jock and black stud. Despite the various opinions surrounding the use of black athletes in advertising, there are still plenty of black men running, jumping, catching, and throwing in advertising today.

Athletic prowess isn't the only ethnic image advertising has borrowed from African American culture. Black images are often used in advertising to convey what is considered "hip," "cool," trendy, and rebellious.

Likewise, Hispanic culture has seeped slowly into the advertising and marketing mainstream. In addition to using visual images, advertisers take advantage of items with a distinctly Latino flavor to distinguish and position their products. This technique has been effective for a number of products. For the first time ever in 1991, picante sauce outsold catsup as the nation's number one condiment. Taco Bell ran for the border in a commercial with an obviously Southwestern theme. McDonald's introduced breakfast fajitas in 1991, and the image of Juan Valdez graces all cans of Colombian coffee. The Latin sound can be heard in the background of Pepsi commercials.

"Hispanic cultural images are not used in mainstream advertising as much as black images because they are not always so readily identifiable," according to Marta Miyares, president of Unimar Communications, a Hispanic advertising agency with offices in Chicago. "Black images are immediately identifiable, making them more desirable for a 30-second spot."[13]

Asian images are also used in advertising, but not with the same frequency as black and Hispanic themes. Mainstream advertising is still struggling with ways to incorporate Asian American culture into its messages. Instead, it often uses native Asians as tourists visiting America, as angry frustrated competitors, or as rich businessmen trying to buy up the nation's precious treasures. In areas with heavy Asian American populations, such as California, distinctly Asian actors and themes are more widely used.

Native American culture is not often used in advertising, but when it has been, it has sometimes offended the audience. The Kansas City Chiefs football team dressed defensive star Derrick Thomas in an Indian warrior headdress for a promotional poster. The Indian community was outraged because the headdress is to be worn only by those who have earned the status of warrior.

In 1984, Chrysler launched a television spot urging car shoppers to buy American (it didn't work) with the theme "The Pride Is Back—Born in America." The ad contained a brief close-up to a Native American in full headdress looking proudly onto the horizon.

To the dismay of many Native Americans, a brewer planned to introduce a new malt liquor called "Crazy Horse" in 1992. The product was obviously named for the legendary Sioux nation chief, but his ancestors claim Crazy Horse despised alcohol because he viewed it as destructive to his people.

Ironically, ethnic images and sounds, so pervasive in today's advertising, are most often used to sell products to mainstream customers. Whether the same approaches and techniques used on the general market are transferable to ethnic consumers is an issue with which the industry is still grappling.

The Role of Ethnic Advertising Agencies

Ethnic advertising agencies, that is, firms with specific expertise in designing ads for minority audiences, have been in existence less than 40 years. Despite a growing interest in the marketplace, ethnic agencies have not flourished like their general market counterparts. According to the 1993 listings in the Standard Directory of Advertising Agencies, 105 firms specialized exclusively or in part with ethnic markets.[14] Of that number, 24 reported expertise in dealing with the African American market, 12 worked with the Asian market, and 69 dealt with Hispanic consumers and products.[15]

These agencies are generally smaller and less competitive than white agencies and thus are more vulnerable to economic downturns. The combined 1991 annual billings for black firms were $300 million—a small sum when compared with billings for Ogilvy and Mather, reported at $5.3 billion for the same year.[16] No ethnic-owned and -operated agency was listed among the top 100 advertising firms in 1993. The 100th largest U.S. agency earned $115 million compared with $77 million billed by the Burrell Communications Group—the largest African American agency.[17]

Ethnic-owned and -operated agencies also suffer from a perception that all they can do is create advertising for ethnic audiences, which may prevent some major marketers from giving them business.

Ethnic agencies tend to disagree with the perception that they are one-dimensional. According to Tom Burrell, chairman and CEO of the Burrell Communications Group:

> We provide clients with several unique services. First, we understand the nuances of black culture and psychology. Second, we can prevent clients from making major mistakes in creative strategy. And, third, because we were the leaders in segmenting the market, we understand how to dissect and penetrate any target audience.[18]

Possibly, the first black-owned full-service agency in the country was Vince Cullers Advertising, founded in 1956. The Chicago-based agency's philosophy was and is "to create advertising that moves clients to their strategic positions."[19] Like its general market counterparts, the agency specializes in marketing and advertising planning, research, creative development, media planning, merchandising, and public relations. Cullers's client list includes such marketers as Amoco Oil, Sears, Kellogg, and Pizza Hut. Annual billings in 1993 were $18 million.[20]

Tom Burrell's advertising agency, founded in 1971, has grown into the nation's largest black-owned agency. The company, now called the Burrell Communications Group, includes three operating units: Burrell Advertising, Burrell Public Relations, and Burrell Consumer Promotions. It is the only black-owned agency with its own building, located on Michigan Avenue in Chicago. It also has offices in Atlanta, Georgia, and employs over 100 people. Burrell's mission is to "employ the highest standards of excellence in designing programs that get results from various market segments."[21] He does not call his firm an ethnic agency. He prefers to call his company a full-service agency specializing in advertising targeted to special markets. The agency has an impressive list of Fortune 500 accounts including the Ford Motor Company, McDonald's, Kmart, Polaroid, First Chicago Corporation, and Quaker Oats.

Keith Lockhart and Tom Pettus opened their New York advertising agency in 1977. The company reported billings of $25 million in 1993.[22] Their clients have included the ROTC, Chrysler, Panasonic, and Consolidated Edison of New York.

The Lockhart and Pettus style is built on reality-based advertising that incorporates what the audience understands with what the product can offer them. Their campaigns are subtle, sophisticated, and empathic. For example, in an ROTC ad aimed at black students attending historically black colleges and universities (HBCUs), the headline reads, "I came for the fellowship, but stayed for the leadership." The advertisement addresses the anxiety some black students feel about attending a black institution by clearly demonstrating the advantages of friendship and professional development.

Lockhart and Pettus's ad campaign for Canadian Club featured an elegantly dressed black couple enjoying the brand and ignoring the rest of the world. The agency used a black saxophonist in a Wendy's ad to impart a jazzy image for the product.

The late Frank Mingo and Caroline Jones also went into business in 1977. They created the "We do chicken right" slogan for KFC and provided services for Pepsi Cola and Disney. After the death of Mingo, the company split into the Mingo Group, with 1993 billings of almost $53 million,[23] and Caroline Jones Advertising, Inc., with billings of $14 million for the same year.[24]

UniWorld Group opened its doors in 1969. The company, located in New York, represents Seven-Up, Burger King, Hueblein's Smirnoff, RCA, AT&T, Coors, and Lincoln Mercury. The agency was awarded the Burger King account in 1983 as a result of an Operation PUSH (People United to Save Humanity) minority contract program; however, it makes no excuses for receiving a client through an affirmative action program. "That might be why we got the business, but it's not why we keep it," said Valerie Graves, senior vice president and creative director.[25] The UniWorld philosophy is simple—always show black consumers in positive situations. The agency says it rejects concepts in which the featured models are depicted in stereotypical settings. With billings nearing $73 million, it is second only to Burrell Advertising.[26] UniWorld Group also has a Hispanic division whose clients include Kodak, Home Box Office (HBO), and Lincoln Mercury.

Hispanic advertising agencies began to emerge in the mid-1980s, and they have flourished rapidly. Most of the nearly 70 firms are located in New York, Florida, California, and Texas, areas with the highest concentration of Hispanic Americans. One of the largest is Conill Advertising, based in New

York, founded by a husband and wife team and now owned by Carlos Rossi. Their 1993 billings were $40 million,[27] and their client list includes McDonald's and Scott Paper.

Conill's strength is sensitivity and imagination in reaching the Hispanic market. The firm uses strong family images in many of its advertisements. A McDonald's campaign Conill called "Our Latin Friendship" showed a Hispanic and an Anglo family coming together at the restaurant. Despite their differences, the two families had one thing in common.

The agency founded by Muse, Cordero, and Chen specializes in advertising to African American, Hispanic, and Asian markets. Located in Los Angeles, the firm reported 1993 billings of $27 million.[28] Its major clients include Nike, Honda Motor Company, Anheuser-Busch Companies, and Home Savings of America. In 1991 the agency was awarded a $7 million contract from Nike, to help the company respond to criticism surrounding its perceived lack of support for ethnic communities.

The largest of the 10 Asian agencies listed in the Standard Directory of Advertising Agencies is AdLand Advertising, San Francisco. Its billings for 1993 were $12.8 million.[29] Others include Pacific Rim Advertising of Los Angeles (1993 billings of $400 thousand),[30] Time Advertising in San Francisco, ($1 million),[31] and L[3] Advertising and Public Relations of New York ($3.3 million).[32]

Competing with major market firms is a big problem for the ethnic agencies. If the Best Awards given by *Advertising Age* are any indication, it is difficult for ethnic agencies to get recognition for their efforts. The magazine honors ads judged on the basis of "creativity."[33] None of the 1991, 1992, or 1993 winners was produced by ethnic-owned agencies; however, the magazine did mention that 1991 entries included ads featuring Hammer, Bo Jackson, David Robinson, Michael Jordan, Ray Charles, Whitney Houston, James Earl Jones, and Spike Lee.[34] In 1991, an ad for HBO starring former heavyweight boxer George Foreman was a winner.[35]

In 1977, the World Institute of Black Communications (WIBC) established the Communications Excellence to Black Audiences (CEBA) Awards Program to honor those advertisements and individuals who "recognize the value of human dignity, cultural differences and ethnic pride in marketing to African American consumers."[36] Each year the organization honors advertisements, public relations campaigns, and public service announcements with awards of excellence, distinction, and merit. There are 47 categories including magazine, outdoor, print, and television.

Ethnic agencies have experienced some growth over the past few decades, but their survival is contingent on their ability to provide unique services and results for the clients. "The advertising industry is in the midst of a huge fallout," Burrell says. "Only the best of the bunch will survive."[37]

DISCUSSION QUESTIONS ◄-------------------------------

1. Do you believe that ethnic advertising is a passing fad, or has it become a permanent part of the advertising business? Why or why not?
2. As advertising budgets decrease, are marketers likely to spend more or less money on ethnic audiences?
3. Should ethnic agencies attempt to compete with mainstream agencies for general market business? What would be the advantages and/or disadvantages of doing so?

Endnotes

1. U.S. Department of Commerce, Bureau of the Census, *Current Population Reports, Population Projections of the United States by Age, Sex, Race and Hispanic Origin: 1993–2050* (November 1993): P-25-1104.
2. Ibid.
3. Mark Landler, Walecia Konrad, Zachary Schiller, and Lois Therrien, "What Happened to Advertising?" *Business Week* (September 23, 1991): 67.
4. Ibid., 66–72.
5. Courtland L. Bovee and William F. Arens, *Contemporary Advertising* (Homewood, Ill.: Richard D. Irwin, Inc., 1989), 49.
6. Landler, Konrad, Schiller, and Therrien, "What Happened to Advertising?" 68.
7. Ibid.
8. Harold W. Berkman and Christopher C. Gilson, *Consumer Behavior Concepts and Strategies* (Encino, Calif.: Dickenson Publishing Co., Inc., 1978), 122.
9. Susan L. Fry, "Reaching Hispanic Publics with Special Events," *Public Relations Journal* 47, no. 2 (February 1991): 12.
10. Ibid.
11. Byron Lewis, interview by Gail Baker Woods, at UniWorld Headquarters, New York, July 30, 1992.
12. London International Advertising Awards, *1990 Television/Cinema Competition Winners*, New York.
13. Marta Miyares, interview by Gail Baker Woods, at Unimar Headquarters, Chicago, Ill., August 12, 1992.
14. Standard Directory of Advertising Agencies, no. 229, July 1993. National Register Publishing Company, New Providence, New Jersey, xxi–xxix.
15. Ibid., xxi.
16. Ibid., xxi–xxvi.
17. Standard Directory of Advertising Agencies.
18. Tom Burrell, interview by Gail Baker Woods, at Burrell Building, Chicago, Ill., March 12, 1992.
19. Vince Cullers, interview by Gail Baker Woods, at Cullers Advertising, Chicago, Ill., August 12, 1992.

20. Standard Directory of Advertising Agencies, 167.
21. Burrell interview.
22. Standard Directory of Advertising Agencies, 433.
23. Ibid., 503.
24. Ibid., 271.
25. Valerie Graves, interview by Nileeni Meegama, UniWorld, New York, March 20, 1993.
26. Standard Directory of Advertising Agencies, 719.
27. Ibid., 148.
28. Ibid., 514.
29. Ibid., 11.
30. Ibid., 549.
31. Ibid., 707.
32. Ibid., 403.
33. "Advertising Age, The Best Awards of 1991," *Advertising Age* (March 30, 1992): 18–23.
34. "Advertising Age, The Best Awards of 1990," *Advertising Age* (March 18, 1991): 24–26.
35. "Advertising Age, The Best Awards of 1991."
36. Adriane Gaines, interview by Gail Baker Woods, at CEBA, New York, July 30, 1992.
37. Burrell interview.

The Evolution of Ethnic Advertising

2

This chapter looks at the roots of ethnic advertising. The evolution of ethnic advertising from the early days of door-to-door sales to the sophisticated techniques employed today is explored. The chapter introduces the major ethnic groups targeted by marketers today and offers a broad description of each.

At the end of this chapter, you should be able to do the following:

1. Identify the pioneers of ethnic advertising
2. Understand some of the ways in which advertising can offend ethnic audiences
3. Discuss how ethnic advertising influences mainstream advertising
4. Cite examples, other than the ones listed, in which the advertiser was insensitive to the concerns of ethnic audiences

➤ The Early Days

Madam C. J. Walker had the right idea in 1900. Long before consumer behavior became a legitimate science, decades before it was fashionable to target specific segments of the marketplace, prior to the onset of strategic marketing plans, Madam Walker, an African American beautician, manufactured beauty products to remove the curl from black hair. Less than 20 years later she was the nation's first self-made female millionaire.[1]

Without the benefit of education, research, or demographic and psychographic data, Madam Walker launched one of the first comprehensive advertising and marketing campaigns aimed at ethnic audiences. By doing so, she became the pioneer in ethnic marketing. Her accomplishments in the areas of segmentation, advertising, and promotion remain unparalleled to this day.

Madam Walker, the daughter of sharecroppers and a former laundress, relied on instinct and mother wit to creatively use all elements of what is now called the marketing mix's four P's (product, price, place, and promotion) in selling her products.

First, she designed a simple product that appealed to her consumers' basic social and psychological needs—a desire to belong and a need to assimilate into mainstream America. African American people believed if they could straighten their curly hair, they could wear the fashionable hairstyles of the day and thus be more acceptable to the mainstream.

Before the introduction of the straightening comb, African American women ironed their hair or wrapped it tightly with string to give it a smoother appearance. The results were often disastrous, including burns and hair loss. Understanding the trouble these women encountered in styling their hair, Madam Walker cleverly positioned the product as a convenient, easy-to-use, safe beauty aid.

The price of the product was inexpensive enough for the market to afford, but not so low that they perceived it to be cheap. Although her audience had very little disposable income, they were willing to spend extra money on products that enhanced their self-esteem.

She placed her product in beauty shops, usually located in the kitchens of the beauticians' small apartments. She also used door-to-door salespersons to introduce the product to consumers who could not afford a beautician, and she employed word of mouth and third-party endorsements to promote the product. Beauticians and hairstylists were happy to spread the news to their customers. They could use the hot comb to attain a totally different and much more desirable look. Singing star and black female role model Josephine Baker, who was living in Europe at the time, heard of the product and began using it on her hair.

Ethnic media were also used as outlets for Madam Walker's hair products. Because African Americans faithfully read black newspapers, she ran ads for her revolutionary straightening comb in publications like the *Pittsburgh Courier* and the *Amsterdam News*. She began with small advertisements, featuring pictures of the products. Her likeness appeared on the jar so that consumers could see it was developed by a black woman. They could take pride in her accomplishments as they purchased the products. By 1911, Madam Walker's company was grossing over $100,000 per year from her hair products.[2]

Madam Walker's marketing ingenuity didn't end with her unique promotional skills. She also employed public relations techniques in her business. She made donations to the National Association for the Advancement of Colored People (NAACP), black orphanages, the Colored YMCA, and educational institutions. It was her belief that a successful company should be a good corporate citizen and offer support to the community in which it operated. She built her own block-long factory in Indianapolis, complete with a barber and beauty shop, and provided jobs for literally hundreds of African Americans. She trained beauticians in how to use the products and then created a new name for graduates of her beauty schools. Instead of being called "hair straighteners," they were promoted as "beauty culturalists."

When she died in 1919, Madam Walker left a fortune of over $1 million. Unbeknownst to her, she also left behind a blueprint on how to market effectively to ethnic audiences.

Less than 15 years after the straightening comb was introduced, the Ad Club of El Paso, Texas, heard a presentation from Silvestre Terrazas on "How to Advertise Among Mexican People."[3] Like Walker, the Mexican newspaper editor was ahead of his time. He spoke of diversity within the Mexican community, the importance of using Spanish-language newspapers to reach the audience, and the need for product manufacturers to develop and maintain good will and customer loyalty.[4] Terrazas told the advertising men that a good product, advertised in a good newspaper, in a good market is what brings progress to the commercial world. Further, he told the audience that Mexicans respond to advertisers who address them in good faith and that promotional items help build and maintain product identity and brand loyalty.[5]

Both Walker and Terrazas approached the topic of ethnic marketing with remarkable clarity and simplicity. They realized that racial and ethnic differences existed that should not be ignored by marketers. They recognized the

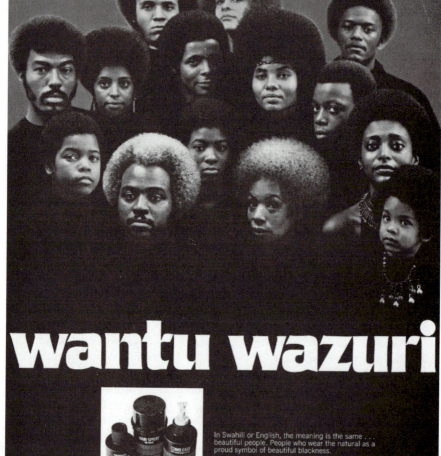

Courtesy Cullers Advertising.

importance of ethnic media in reaching the target audience. They believed advertising, public relations, and the marketing mix were effective tools if used with cultural sensitivity and an understanding of the target audience.

Yet, almost a century later, mainstream marketers continue to grapple with how to advertise and market to ethnic subcultures. Many ignore the principles so eloquently demonstrated by the early target marketers and look for new solutions to questions that, in many cases, have already been answered. They employ some of the best research minds and use the most sophisticated techniques to help them penetrate the ethnic market. However, many of them still make elementary mistakes. The results are classic and haunting examples of insensitivity, botched product plans, boycotts, and backlashes. In short, many of today's mega-marketers fail to recognize some basic facts about how ethnic consumers differ from their white counterparts.

Some modern marketers attempt to transfer mainstream images to ethnic advertising without considering how they might offend and alienate consumers. Others ignore potentially lucrative market segments altogether because of misconceptions about the market's growth and viability. Despite their best efforts, some firms generate considerable negative publicity around their products, which infuriates the exact audience they are trying to woo.

Changes in Ethnic Advertising

It wasn't until the late 1940s that consumer behavior became recognized as a science. Since then, an impressive body of literature on target marketing, demographics, and social and cultural segmentation has developed. Motivational research (that is, the hidden reasons behind why people purchase products and services) was developed in the 1950s. With the 1960s came more in-depth research about the psychology of advertising.

During the early years of consumer behavior research, ethnic audiences were virtually ignored. Researchers in the "new" field concentrated their efforts on the "average American," a term not associated with ethnic minorities. The ethnic population was steadily growing, but marketing research simply was not keeping pace with it.

By the end of the 1960s, there was new interest in ethnic audiences. The Civil Rights Bill and more educational opportunities for African Americans led marketers to view them as a potentially lucrative audience.

Textbooks began to discuss ethnic subcultures in the 1960s, but clearly, many of them misunderstood the power and diversity of this up-and-coming group. In a 1968 consumer behavior text by Engel, Kollat, and Blackwell, the authors describe the "Negro" subculture as follows:

1. Negroes save more money than whites of equivalent incomes, have more careful purchasing habits, and take the purchase of products more seriously than equivalent whites.
2. Upper-class Negroes have less social contact than equivalent whites.
3. Fashion-conscious Negroes rely on the mass media, especially white fashion magazines.
4. Negro women are more likely to shop with other woman than their husbands in contrast to white patterns where women shop with their husbands.
5. Negroes appear to be more brand loyal than equivalent whites.
6. Negroes dislike purchasing products that are symbols reminding them of their historical slavery or inferior social position.
7. Negroes tend to purchase more luxury items than white consumers of the same income level.
8. The wife occupies the dominant position in the economic decision making of the Negro family.[6]

The information the authors provide must be viewed in the context of the time in which it was published. Few comprehensive studies on the African American subculture had been conducted; therefore, limited data were available. However, there had been a considerable amount of research on subcultures within mainstream America that the marketing experts might have applied to the African American market. Demographic data on the sex, age, income, and educational levels of consumers were being used to segment the market into defined categories. Nonetheless, market researchers continued to lump all African Americans into one market. No mention was made of the differences among African Americans in terms of their education, social class, status, age, or family structure. All "Negroes" were perceived to be the same: Supposedly, they aspired to the same goals, came from the same backgrounds, and desired the same products.

In 1970, Milton Gordon made an effort to bring credence to the role of ethnic subcultures. In his article "The Subsociety and the Subculture," he described three important functions of ethnic subcultures:

1. To provide a psychological source of group identification
2. To offer a patterned network of groups and institutions
3. To serve as a frame of reference for viewing the new culture[7]

In 1979, Kelvin Wall, in his article "Trying to Reach the Black Market? Beware of Marketing Myopia," made a startling discovery. He stated:

> A decade ago, the typical successful black adopted the white man's middle-class style. The black from Tuskegee was more Ivy League than the Brahmin from Yale. Blacks are no longer emulating whites. They are expressing their black consciousness. More important, they are not monolithic. They are using different products to differentiate among themselves.[8]

In 1979, McAdoo studied the "new" black middle class, those with average incomes of $33,000. She found significant differences among the group in terms of lifestyle, buying behavior, and education. In fact, McAdoo found that in many cases, black middle-class consumer buying patterns were not much different from those of whites.[9] Her research, published in *Psychology Today*, produced the first known profile of the black middle class.

Mellott, in his 1983 text on consumer behavior, came to a similar conclusion about differences within the black marketplace: ". . . as we have seen in our discussion of income, education, and the black middle class, the black market is as diverse as the white market."[10]

The Hispanic market became the subject of interest and study in the 1970s, when its numbers began to increase substantially. Burma, in the 1978 Berkman and Gilson text of consumer behavior, described the Mexican American subculture this way:

> There is a growing middle-class among second- and third-generation Mexican-Americans—and evidence that those who have achieved educational success, higher status occupations and other requirements of middle-class social acceptance experience little or no overt discrimination.[11]

By the mid-1980s, marketers were beginning to recognize the potential of Hispanic consumers but were still baffled about how to penetrate the market. In 1983, Mellott made the following observation:

> A majority of Spanish families emigrated from a comparatively simple economy in which culture and tradition dominate behavior. . . . Because of the language problem, the Spanish-American market . . . is difficult to reach. It is highly individual in choices, not only of products but also of brands.[12]

The Asian American market did not gain prominence until the 1980s, the decade following unprecedented growth in its numbers. The population grew by 42 percent between 1970 and 1980 and is expected to increase another 165 percent between 1990 and 2000.[13] The segment has been called the "Sleeping Dragon" and the "Super Minority." It is a small market, compared with African Americans and Hispanics. Nevertheless, because of its relative affluence, the Asian American market has become fertile territory for product marketers. Like Hispanics, Asian Americans are a fragmented group composed of autonomous subcomponents including Japanese, Chinese, Koreans, Filipinos, and Vietnamese.

Cultural heritages steeped in tradition and surrounded by mystery present significant obstacles for marketers who often find the customs, behaviors, and consumption patterns of Asians puzzling. Confounding the problem is a lack of research and timely information on Asian American consumer behavior and lifestyles. For the time being, few firms specialize in marketing to Asian Americans, and few advertising campaigns are aimed directly at them.

Native Americans, too, have been nonexistent to marketers, possibly a result of their relatively small numbers and isolation from the American mainstream. Native American images are often used by advertisers, but few of the products marketed are targeted at this audience.

⟩ Ethnic Images in Advertising

From the late 1970s to the present, there has been a burgeoning body of literature on ethnic advertising and marketing. Some of the studies focused on the number of ethnic images in advertising; others looked at the effect of advertising on minority audiences, and still others examined how ethnic minorities are portrayed in advertising.

Advertising designed to attract ethnic audiences and advertising that features ethnic images are two distinct issues that need to be clearly delineated. The former is a function of strategic marketing aimed at a specific target audience. The latter is a social responsibility issue, that is, the role of advertisers and their agencies in fostering realistic images of all segments of the population. However, the two functions are inextricably linked in terms of understanding what techniques work in reaching the ethnic target audience.

Before the social responsibility aspect of advertising is discussed, it is important to review the role of ethnic images in advertising. The subject of how often ethnic groups are used in advertising has been studied by a number of researchers with mixed results. In 1969, Kassarjian wrote:

> . . . the ads that treat the Negro as an equal are so few that the civil rights groups cannot be acclaimed successful nor can the advertising industry take particular pride in their supposedly newly found social responsibility.[14]

According to Gould, Sigband, and Zoerner, marketers who used ads featuring black models risked backlash from white consumers. They went on to say that evidence of this backlash has not been demonstrated.[15] Without the benefit of empirical data to substantiate their fears, advertisers avoided black models throughout the 1950s. Despite his popularity as an entertainer, balladeer Nat King Cole (father of songstress Natalie Cole) could not find a national sponsor for his 1956 television show. It was not until 1960 that he became one of the first blacks to appear in network television commercials. Others celebrities, like Lena Horne and Bill Cosby, followed Cole. Although today there is no doubt that there is more minority representation in advertising, the issues of how they are portrayed and what they contribute to the product's image remain controversial.

Marketing communications research has demonstrated the effectiveness of source credibility on the persuasive influence over the message receiver. Specifically, interaction among the variables of source, message, and receiver has been extensively studied. Mellott and others call source credibility the most important characteristic in persuasion. Credibility is enhanced when the message receiver holds a favorable attitude toward the source, when the receiver perceives similarity between the source and himself or herself, and when the source is likable.[16]

The subject of using ethnic images to improve communication and persuasion directed toward ethnic audiences has been studied by a number of researchers with contradictory results.

Gould, Sigband, and Zoerner's 1970 study, "Black Consumer Reaction to 'Integrated' Advertising," looked at the effect of black or white models on subject receptivity. They found no evidence that blacks react more favorably to ads with black models.[17]

Muse reported similar findings. In his study conducted on black college students, Muse found that ads using black models were rated as favorably as ads with white models. He did note that cigarette ads with black models were rated higher by the group than ads with white models. For feminine hygiene products, the group judged ads featuring white models more favorably.[18]

Some marketers interpreted these results to mean that there was no empirical evidence to support using black models to reach black audiences. This reasoning was flawed for several reasons. To begin with, the early researchers did not take into account the effect of racism and stereotypical imagery on the subjects at the time the studies were conducted.

Ken Smikle, publisher of *Target Market News*, a newsletter aimed at businesses trying to reach black audiences, said that centuries of social and economic hardship created low self-esteem for black people in this culture. As a result, black people began to believe that anything associated with whites was better than anything associated with blacks.[19] He further explained that whites would have more credibility with the subjects than blacks because the perception was that whites were having better lives, had been exposed to more, and simply knew more about products than blacks did.

Another explanation for Muse's findings was the infrequency with which African Americans actually saw black people in advertising. Before Muse's study, Kassarjian reported that only one-third of 1 percent of all integrated advertising featured any black people. It is possible that the subjects had been conditioned to associating effective message delivery with white models.[20]

More recent research into the use of ethnic models on the communication of persuasive messages has revealed findings to support the theory that minorities prefer to see images of people like themselves in advertising. Therefore, it is reasonable to assume that advertising aimed at ethnic audiences should feature ethnic models because their similarity to the consumers lends credibility to the product. However, such a straightforward approach is fraught with caveats if the marketers do not understand the nuances of ethnic culture. "Simply replacing white faces with ethnic faces is a mistake," according to Keith Lockhart, managing partner of Lockhart and Pettus, New York. "Some concepts and images are not transferable across cultures," he added.[21]

Tom Burrell described the popular McDonald's "You deserve a break today" advertising campaign of the 1970s as an example of cultural differences that affect advertising. "Because most inner-city McDonald's restaurants are located within walking distance from their homes, black families dine there often—sometimes more than once a day. The inference that going to McDonald's was a special treat did not wash with black consumers."[22] Burrell changed the campaign for black consumers to "McDonald's sure is good to have around."

The Burrell agency also changed the themeline in a 1974 Coke ad campaign from "Look up America and see what you've got" to "For the real times, it's the real thing." Burrell said the concept was altered because in 1974 black people had yet to feel as though they could take pride in America. In his opinion, black consumers might have found the original themeline offensive, and thus, they might have rejected the campaign and the product outright.

UniWorld, a New York-based black-owned advertising agency, modified a general market theme for Smirnoff, a premium liquor produced by Heublein. The brand had been using the line "Friends are good to have around." According to Valerie Graves, senior vice president and creative director at UniWorld, the theme was changed because black people don't, as a rule, serve a premium brand of liquor to show friends they're worth something. "We serve premium liquor to show them we have very good taste," she said. "Seal the friendship" became the brand's new campaign line.[23]

Most researchers agree that there has been considerable growth in the use of ethnic models in ads. Modifying or changing advertising themes rather than just "coloring" them has become a popular trend accompanying the increased number of minorities represented in advertising.

It is more difficult to ascertain if, with more ethnic faces, there have been any substantial changes in how minorities are portrayed. In other words, are more ethnic images actually better images, or do they support age-old stereotypes? The issue of ad imagery is important in the study of advertising because through the use of visuals and sounds we are able to see how the dominant culture views subcultures.

In his 1969 ground-breaking research, Kassarjian reported that the role portrayals of black and black–white interaction increased over the period 1946–1965.[24] Cox later found that there was an increase in the total number of ads portraying African Americans and that black role portrayals switched from unskilled-oriented in 1949 to skilled-oriented in 1968.[25]

In an effort to measure both quantity and quality of ethnic advertising, Colfax and Sternberg analyzed *Readers Digest, Life, Look,* and *Ladies Home*

Journal.[26] They found that the number of blacks appearing in the magazines increased in the 1960s, but the manner in which they were depicted tended to confirm and perpetuate racial stereotypes. Conversely, in 1986, Zinkhan, Cox, and Hong found what they called "improvements" in the occupational status of black models in magazine advertisements.[27]

When Bush, Solomon, and Hair examined the role of blacks in television advertising, in 1974, they concluded the following:

1. There was an increase in the use of black models between 1967 and 1974.
2. Black models were more likely to be found in public service announcements (PSAs).
3. When present in product ads, black models were more likely to advertise personal products like hair care versus nonpersonal products, such as automobiles.[28]

More recently, in the Zinkhan, Qualls, and Biswas study, the researchers concluded that black representation had increased over time and that blacks were more often represented in television than in print advertising.[29]

Reid and Vanden Bergh examined at what stage of the product life cycle African Americans were used in advertising. They found that despite evidence of an increased effort by advertisers to integrate African Americans into their advertising, there was no clear trend in the use of African Americans in introductory magazine ads.[30] The researchers did find what they called an "upgrade" in the characterization of African Americans in advertising from background roles to minor roles, but no substantial change in major roles. They also found that when African American models appeared in introductory advertising, they were more likely to be used in the selling of personal care products.

Further, the researchers reported that during the introductory phase of a product, when expenditures were high and profits low, African Americans were used in only 0.68 percent of advertising. Of the 8,700 introductory ads they surveyed, 59 featured blacks.[31] These results led them to conclude the following:

1. Advertisers are hesitant to use blacks in introductory ads because the research on consumer responses to integrated advertising is inconclusive.
2. Blacks are less likely to appear in introductory advertisements because they are less likely than whites to adopt innovative and new products.[32]

These findings fly in the face of what black agencies know about black audiences, according to Adriane Gaines, executive director of CEBA, an organization that gives annual awards to advertisers for promoting positive African American images.

> Maybe black people don't adopt innovations because they create them. It's no secret that black people are often the first to develop new music, rap, for example;

are more likely to start fashion trends like dread locks and kinte cloth; and were eating chicken wings long before the fast food operations started selling them.[33]

Burrell calls the lack of use of minorities in introductory ads a mistake. According to him:

> . . . the use of blacks in advertising grabs attention of both black and white viewers, but for different reasons. Some blacks may pay attention to the ad because it has music or features a person or subject with which they can relate. Others look at the ad because they are fearful of what they might see. They may approach the ad with an "Uh-oh, what are they going to say about us now," attitude. Either way, they're paying attention—which is what you want your advertising to accomplish.[34]

Burrell said whites and others will pay attention to an ad featuring blacks because of their interest in and curiosity about black culture. Valerie Graves, of UniWorld Group, agrees: ". . . so much of popular culture is really black in origin."[35]

Despite what the black advertising executives cite as positive aspects of minority images, advertisers have been reluctant to include them in many of their campaigns. In 1985, the Lawyers Committee for Civil Rights Under Law attacked the *Washington Post* Real Estate section for a sparsity of minorities featured in its display advertising. From January 1985 through April 1986, minorities were featured in less than 2 percent of the *Post*'s ads, according to Kerry Scanlon, attorney for the Washington-based Lawyers Committee.[36] At the time, the population of Washington, D.C., was 90 percent black. The *Post* responded by setting a 25 percent target for African Americans in display ads. The paper further said it would refuse advertising that didn't comply with the policy.

In 1990, the New York City Department of Consumer Affairs found that only 3 percent of people in national advertising were black, causing Mark Green, Consumer Office commissioner, to state, "This racial neglect is both economically dumb and morally offensive. What we see affects what we think."[37] The commission cited *Esquire, Vogue,* and *Gentlemen's Quarterly* as the worst offenders. On the flip side, it said *Sports Illustrated* advertising featured the most blacks. The report went on to say that when blacks appear in ads, they are often athletes, entertainers, laborers, or children.

If the incidence of blacks in general is low in ads, it's even lower for black women. Less than 20 percent of all ads with blacks feature black women. When they are seen, black women are often portrayed as "jive"-talking, sassy "sisters" or overweight, wise-cracking, church-going women. For example, there was a controversial Roy Rogers commercial, in which a black female restaurant manager is seen scolding the TV viewer. She says, "I can't stand to see eatin' as much as a leg anywhere but Roy Rogers." In another example, a fruit juice ad features three overweight black women expressing incredulity at the notion of combining unlikely flavors into a beverage. Between the three of them, a complete sentence is never uttered. A middle-aged African American woman embarrassed her husband by discussing his constipation with a total stranger. Another overweight black woman shocked her daughter by reminding her of the stomachache she suffered the night before.

African Americans have fared poorly in advertising, but Hispanics have done even worse. Hispanic Americans were practically nonexistent in advertising before 1980. A decade later one study found Hispanic models were only 1.5 percent of the speaking characters on network television ads.[38]

The underrepresentation of ethnic models in advertising has implications beyond marketing strategy. There are social and psychological issues as well. Because the mainstream society develops many of its views about ethnic groups through advertising and other media, stereotypical representations can lead to stereotypical attitudes.

Wilkes and Valencia go so far as to say that ethnic stereotypes portrayed in advertising actually interfere with the acculturation and assimilation process of ethnic minorities.[39] In their examination of how ethnic minorities were portrayed in advertising, they looked at three major categories:

1. Major roles, that is, roles very important to the commercial theme or layout, in which the person is shown in the foreground and/or holding the product and/or appears to be speaking
2. Minor roles, that is, roles of average importance to the commercial theme or layout in which the person does not appear to be speaking
3. Background roles, that is, roles that are hard to find, and are not important to the commercial theme or layout

Of the 904 commercials viewed, Hispanics were judged to appear in only 53, or 5.8 percent. Hispanics were usually perceived as unimportant to the commercials, appearing primarily in background roles and as part of a group. They were seen more often in commercials for food products, entertainment, alcohol, and furniture.[40]

Blacks appeared in 17 percent of the commercials viewed and were judged to have major roles in 31 percent of the ads in which they appeared. Like Hispanics, blacks tend to appear in groups, but the groups were smaller (an average of 6.9 persons) for blacks than for Hispanics (an average of 8.1 persons per group). Blacks were most likely to appear in food, automobile, liquor, electronic products, and hair care product commercials.[41]

Therefore, although it is clear that there are more ethnic minorities in commercials, whether their roles are representative of the wide range of activities in which they participate is inconclusive.

Despite the promulgation of ethnic sounds and images in advertising, little attention is paid to stereotypes in advertising textbooks. A random review of textbooks found that they offer little or no insight into how to develop special market advertising, how to use ethnic media, and how to avoid stereotypical portrayals.

Ethnic audiences have often been overlooked and misunderstood by the advertising industry, researchers, and academics. Consequently, stereotypes have emerged about what ethnic consumers like to see and how they will respond to commercial advertising. It is difficult—sometimes impossible—for companies to recover from the serious blunders that result.

Take, for example, the case of the Frito Lay Bandito. In 1967, Foote, Cone and Belding, one of the nation's leading advertising agencies, created a Mexican character to promote Frito Lay products. Far from being a nice guy, the bandit often conned Anglos out of their Fritos. The Mexican American Anti-Defamation Committee didn't like the ad campaign, citing that the character was unshaven, unfriendly, and a negative stereotype. The advertising agency stood by the character because their research indicated that Mexican Americans liked the bandit. But, in 1970, the campaign was withdrawn.

In a more recent example, Young and Rubicam's Bravo Division almost used "polvo Johnson" instead of "talco Johnson" to advertise baby powder. "Polvo" means sexual intercourse in some parts of the Caribbean. When Braniff translated its "Fly in Leather" campaign into Spanish, the slogan emerged as "Fly Naked." Coors Beer wanted drinkers to "Turn it loose tonight." The company dropped the themeline in Spanish, because the translation means "loose bowels." Chicken king Frank Perdue stated, "It takes a tough man to make a tender chicken." The slightly kinky Spanish translation was, "It takes a sexually stimulated man to make a chicken affectionate."

The State of Pennsylvania also learned the hard way. In 1973, the state lottery commission developed a promotion featuring the slogan "No tickee, no money." The Chinese American community was outraged at what they considered an ethnic slur. It served as a reminder of a time when Chinese Americans had difficulty speaking the language and worked as launderers. They were believed to say, "No tickee—no shirtee."

In 1983, the Black Media Association sent letters to a number of advertisers, complaining about what the group called "offensive advertising." They criticized Dow Chemical for a Ziploc commercial in which all the actors had a speaking part except the robust black woman, whose excitement with the product was expressed through the phrase "Ooh-wee!" The commercial looked innocuous enough on the surface, but it reminded some of the portrayal of black women as inarticulate mammies in Hollywood classics like *Gone with the Wind* and *Imitation of Life*. The black "mammy" was generally overweight and subservient and used outbursts, instead of sentences, to express herself.

The watchdogs also cited Central Piedmont Community College for producing and airing a television spot featuring no African Americans, despite a black enrollment of 24 percent. African American students who never visited the campus were led to believe that there was no place for them at the institution.

The Black Media Association was also unhappy with Gallo Winery because of a Thunderbird wine commercial that suggested that middle-class African Americans consumed the product.[42] A short history lesson is required here. In the 1960s poorer, inner-city blacks who were heavy and habitual drinkers preferred Thunderbird wine because it was cheap and potent. Its heavy usage even spawned a children's rhyme.

> What's the word?
> Thunderbird!
> What's the price?
> 50 twice. (one dollar)
> What's the action?
> Satisfaction.
> Who drinks the most?
> Us colored folks.
> Who drinks the less?
> Elliot Ness!

Any suggestion that middle-income African Americans would drink such a product was offensive to this segment of the target audience.

Ronco was also attacked for its Mr. Microphone ad, in which an African American man was shown singing and dancing down a hill. This type of representation is also a throwback to times when blacks were portrayed in Hollywood as minstrels, happy to entertain and serve whites despite their own ignorance, poverty, and lack of status.

Other ads of the 1970s and 1980s offended major segments of the audience. Kraft Foods' 1970s barbeque sauce campaign featured an Uncle Ben type character whose memorable line was "Does yo' cookin' proud." Some members of the audience were bothered the phraseology used to express the major thought. The character could have just as easily said, "You'll be proud of your cooking."

The 1980s also gave us countless images of African Americans as dancers and rappers. Taco Bell launched its "99 cents" campaign of the late 1980s around a 20-something black man searching his pockets for change. He obviously didn't have much money. Since it appeared to be mid-afternoon and he was dressed in jeans and a T-shirt but was nowhere near a college campus, he obviously had no job. But he did have enough money for a taco.

When it began the "Run for the Border" campaign, Taco Bell used a white singer who attempted to imitate black rock and roller Little Richard. Later, the company hired Little Richard himself but still maintained the white singer in their ads. In 1993, Taco Bell developed a new television campaign, in which a group of African "savages" were used to represent "wild" tacos.

Another example of recent portrayals of minorities in advertising is the beer commercial in which two junior executives—one white and one black—open a bottle of beer during lunch and are transported to a tropical paradise where they are surrounded by scantily clad bathing beauties. The black man, apparently seeking approval from his white companion, asks if they should invite the boss next time. His friend, who responds with an emphatic "no," appears to be shocked by such a ridiculous question.

A popular bug spray manufacturer aired a television commercial in which a group of roaches, dressed in untied gym shoes, were assaulted by a woman with a can of bug killer. Her response to their desire to feast on her crumbs was, "Think again, home bug." The statement was an obvious takeoff of a popular African American idiom. "Home boy" is a term used primarily by black males to describe a neighbor or member of one's own community. Unlaced athletic shoes is also a trait most often, although not exclusively, associated with black urban youth. The combination of words and visuals in this ad sent the message that roaches—some of the most disliked, annoying, and dirtiest creatures around—are also black.

These blatant examples of racial insensitivity are easy to identify; however, other advertisers and marketers manage to offend ethnic audiences in more subtle ways. There are sins of omission, like Revlon's 1987 campaign featuring the "World's Most Beautiful Women," with not one ethnic woman included. In 1989, Revlon's "Most Beautiful Woman" was 20-year-old Mary Xinh Nguyen, a Vietnamese American from California.

Hispanics aren't often seen in mainstream advertising drinking coffee, washing dishes, or hosting dinner parties. Asian Americans are often seen through their children, who wear diapers, eat breakfast, and play with toys. But where do these children come from? Who are their parents? One of the first times an Asian couple was prominently featured in a national ad campaign was in the 1970s when a Chinese launderer was fooling his white customers into believing he had some ancient secret for getting their clothes so clean. He was really using Calgon fabric softener.

A television ad for Oreo cookies shows an Asian boy and a Caucasian boy seated side by side in an airport. The Asian boy begins to eat his Oreo, when he is instructed by the Caucasian that his technique is wrong. He should first open the cookie and eat the inside before eating the chocolate outside. It is the white child who understands the "proper" way to eat the cookie.

There are also ad campaigns that were offensive before they even aired. In 1989, the RJ Reynolds Tobacco Company developed a cigarette aimed at black consumers. The company ignored research indicating that 48,000 African Americans died from smoking-related illnesses in 1988.[43] The furor that followed the product announcement caused RJ Reynolds to snatch Uptown from production before it hit the stores, but after the company had invested millions of dollars into its research and development.

Unfortunately, there are numerous negative examples of how ethnic stereotyping is used in advertising. But, in view of the spending power ethnic audiences possess, it is financial suicide for marketers to continue to ignore or offend them.

DISCUSSION QUESTIONS ◄--------------------------------

1. Is all stereotyping negative? Can you think of an example where an advertising stereotype could be used in a positive manner?
2. What should advertisers who receive complaints from ethnic audiences do about the campaigns in question?
3. Do ethnic audiences take advertising too seriously, or should they be offended by certain ads?
4. Black athletes are prominently portrayed in advertising. Does advertising have a responsibility to use other images, like businesspersons and doctors, in their campaigns?

Endnotes

1. *Dictionary of American Negro Biography*, ed. Rayford W. Logan and Michael R. Winston (New York: W.W. Norton and Company, 1982).
2. Charles Latham, Jr., "Madam C. J. Walker and Company," *Traces* (Summer 1989): 29–37.
3. Felix Gutierrez, "Advertising and the Growth of Minority Markets and Media," *Journal of Communication Inquiry* 14, no. 1 (Winter 1990): 6.
4. Ibid.
5. Ibid.
6. James F. Engel, David T. Kollat, and Roger D. Blackwell, *Consumer Behavior*, Holt Rinehart & Winston Marketing Series (New York, San Francisco: Holt, Rinehart & Winston, 1968), 260.
7. Milton Gordon, "The Subsociety and the Subculture" in Arnold, *Sociology of Subcultures*, quoted in Harold W. Berkman and Christopher C. Gilson, *Consumer Behavior Concepts and Strategies* (Encino, Calif.: Dickenson Publishing, 1970), 123.
8. Kelvin A. Wall, "Trying to Reach Blacks? Beware of Marketing Myopia," *Advertising Age* (May 21, 1979), quoted in Douglas W. Mellott, Jr., *Fundamentals of Consumer Behavior* (Tulsa: Pennwell Publishing, 1983), 140.
9. Hariette Piper McAdoo, "Black Kinship," *Psychology Today* (May 1979): 67–70, 79, 110, quoted in Douglas W. Mellott, Jr., *Fundamentals of Consumer Behavior* (Tulsa: Pennwell Publishing, 1983), 131.
10. Douglas W. Mellott, Jr., *Fundamentals of Consumer Behavior* (Tulsa: Pennwell Publishing, 1983), 140.
11. John H. Burma, ed., *Mexican Americans in the United States: A Reader* (Cambridge, Mass.: Schenkman Publishing, 1970), xvi–xvii, quoted in Harold W.

Berkman and Christopher C. Gilson, *Consumer Behavior Concepts and Strategies* (Encino, Calif.: Dickenson Publishing, 1978), 124.

12. Mellott, *Fundamentals of Consumer Behavior*, 122.
13. Richard Kern, "The Asian Market: Too Good to Be True?" *Sales and Marketing Management* (May 1989): 39.
14. Harold H. Kassarjian, "The Negro and American Advertising, 1946–1965," *Journal of Marketing Research* (February 1969): 29–39.
15. John W. Gould, Norman B. Sigband, and Cyril E. Zoerner, Jr., "Black Consumer Reactions to 'Integrated' Advertising: An Exploratory Study," *Journal of Marketing* (July 1970): 20–26.
16. Mellott, *Fundamentals of Consumer Behavior*, 607.
17. Gould, Sigband, and Zoerner, "Black Consumer Reactions to 'Integrated' Advertising."
18. William V. Muse, "Product-Related Response to Use of Black Models in Advertising," *Journal of Marketing Research* 8 (1970):107–109.
19. Ken Smikle, telephone interview by Gail Baker Woods, February 4, 1994.
20. Kassarjian, "The Negro and American Advertising," 32.
21. Keith Lockhart, interview by Gail Baker Woods, Lockhart and Pettus, New York, July 30, 1992.
22. Tom Burrell, interview by Gail Baker Woods, Burrell Building, Chicago, March 12, 1992.
23. Debra Kent, "UniWorld Turns Trend into Crossover Appeal," *Advertising Age* (19 December 1985): 16.
24. Kassarjian, "The Negro and American Advertising," 29–39.
25. Keith K. Cox, "Social Effects of Integrated Advertising," *Journal of Advertising Research* 10 (April 1970): 41–44.
26. J. David Colfax and Susan Frankel Sternberg, "The Perpetuation of Racial Stereotypes: Blacks in Mass Circulation Magazine Advertisements," *Public Opinion Quarterly* 36 (Spring 1972): 8–18.
27. George M. Zinkhan, Keith Cox, and Jae Hong, "Changes in Stereotypes: Blacks and Whites in Magazine Advertisements," *Journalism Quarterly* 63 (1986): 568–572.
28. Ronald F. Bush, Paul Solomon, and Joseph Hair, "There Are More Blacks in Television Commercials," *Journal of Advertising Research* 17 (February 1974): 21–25.
29. George Zinkhan, William Qualls, and Abhijit Biswas, "The Use of Blacks in Magazine and Television Advertising," *Journalism Quarterly* 67 (Autumn 1990): 547.
30. Leonard N. Reid and Bruce G. Vanden Bergh, "Blacks in Introductory Ads," *Journalism Quarterly* 57 (Autumn 1980): 485–488.
31. Ibid.
32. Ibid.
33. Adriane Gaines, interview by Gail Baker Woods, World Institute for Communications, New York, July 30, 1992.
34. Burrell interview.
35. Kent, "UniWorld Turns Trend into Crossover Appeal," 6.
36. "Show More Minorities in Ads: Post," *Advertising Age* (11 August 1986): 3.

37. Pat Guy, "Study Says Ads Overlook Minorities," *USA Today* (24 July 1991): 2B.
38. Robert E. Wilkes and Humberto Valencia, "Hispanics and Blacks in Television Commercials," *Journal of Advertising* 18 (1989): 19–25.
39. Ibid.
40. Ibid.
41. Ibid.
42. Craig Reiss, "Black Media Association Cites Offensive Ads," *Advertising Age* (19 September 1983): 78.
43. Centers for Disease Control, "Smoking-Attributable Mortality and Years of Potential Life Lost—United States, 1988," *Morbidity and Mortality Weekly Report* 36 (1990): 693–697.

Ethnic Consumer Behavior

3

This chapter reviews the consumer behavior of ethnic audiences and discusses how these patterns affect message and campaign development. A brief analysis of the techniques used to gather data about ethnic consumers is included. The role of family, social class, perceptions, and attitudes of ethnic audiences on their consumer behavior is also discussed.

On finishing this chapter, students should have a thorough understanding of the following:

1. How ethnic consumers differ from nonethnic consumers in buying, viewing, reading, and consumption patterns
2. Guidelines for developing advertising and marketing messages aimed at ethnic audiences
3. How marketers can avoid advertising pitfalls by understanding ethnic consumer behavior

Overview of the Marketplace

At the start of the 1990s, there were nearly 32 million African Americans in the United States, with an estimated purchasing power of between $170 and $300 billion.[1] Hispanics, at 24 million people, have an estimated annual purchasing power of $206 billion.[2] The Asian American market, estimated to be 6.5 million,[3] spends $35 billion on consumer products annually.[4]

The Hispanic population is the fastest growing ethnic minority in the nation. It grew from 9 million to 23.7 million between 1970 and 1989.[5] That's an increase of 163 percent! By the year 2010, Hispanics are expected to be the largest minority group in the country, with an estimated 41 million people. The buying power of Hispanic Americans more than tripled from 1980 to 1994, from $60 billion to $206 billion.[6]

The Native American population is the smallest of all minority groups in the United States, estimated at 1.5 million people. They make up less than eight-tenths of 1 percent of the nation's population. Native Americans generally reside on rural reservations and have the lowest median income of all Americans. At least one-third of them live at or below the poverty line.[7] Native Americans are the only ethnic minority group whose numbers are not expected to increase dramatically by the year 2000.

These changes in the marketplace cannot be overlooked. New consumers are emerging and with them come different needs, desires, expectations, and behaviors. Cultural backgrounds influence buying decisions. Consumption patterns shift as family sizes differ. Lifestyles vary from market to market. Messages that do not take into consideration the variations in consumer behavior among ethnic groups could be doomed to failure.

It is important for marketers to understand ethnic markets because these groups provide fertile territory for new consumers. Because some products will fall out of favor with the general population, new markets must be uncovered if the manufacturer is to survive. Cooking oil, for example, is no longer the choice of health-conscious Americans. Cigarettes, too, have become a less popular item among whites. Processed foods, such as canned soup, which is very high in sodium, have lost popularity with some consumers.

Ethnic markets can be lucrative sources of untapped consumer dollars. They are big and growing bigger. They are becoming more affluent, educated, and sophisticated. Some are brand loyal; others are comparison shoppers. There are consumer behaviors common to all ethnic groups and stark contrasts distinguishing them. In some ways, ethnic consumers are much like their nonethnic counterparts. In other ways, they are complex, mysterious, and intriguing. The key to penetrating this potential gold mine is the marketers' knowledge of what works and why.

Profile of African American Consumers

The 32 million African Americans who reside in the United States are likely to spend nearly $889 billion by the year 2000. It is estimated that $700 million is spent annually to reach black consumers.[8]

D. Parke Gibson's 1969 book, *The $30 Billion Negro*, was the first to discuss the African American market in detail. He predicted that personal consumption expenditures for African Americans would increase in the 1980s, and they did.[9]

African American consumers are unique, but they are not very difficult to understand if carefully examined. Unlike any other ethnic minority in this country, African Americans suffered through the horrors of slavery. Whereas Asians and Hispanics immigrate to America seeking a better life, African Americans were brought to this country against their will. The scars of slavery, lynchings, court-ordered discrimination, and denial of basic human rights linger in the African American psyche. To be effective, marketers need to understand how being black in America affects buying behavior, responses to advertising, and consumption patterns.

According to Ken Smikle, publisher of *Target Market News*, African Americans seek products that show they are important members of society. Other advertising executives and researchers agree that, in general, black consumers are still attempting to shake the bonds of slavery, prove their worthiness, and empower themselves through product purchases.[10]

This consumer behavior must be considered against a backdrop of the economic facts facing black people in America. Although African Americans are the oldest and largest minority group in America today, they are near the bottom of the social and economic ladder. The average household income for African Americans in 1990 was $14,051, compared with $16,271 for Hispanics, $21,173 for whites, and $23,671 for Asian Americans.[11]

Black people are less likely than all other groups, except Hispanics, to have completed college, 8.4 and 7.6 percent, respectively.[12] The jobless rate for blacks is consistently the highest in the nation, hovering at about 10 percent. In major urban centers where most African Americans live, unemployment rates higher than the national average have been reported.

Another factor influencing the African African market is the fact that half of all households are headed by females.[13] These families are most likely to live in a cycle of poverty. In fact, 31.3 percent of all African Americans were living below the poverty level at the beginning of the 1990s.[14] On the opposite end of the scale, 10 percent of African Americans have household incomes of $50,000 and above.[15]

Consumer behavior research conducted on African Americans is a relatively new field. Some early investigators made critical errors in interpreting the behavior of this group. In his 1983 book, Mellott cautioned against drawing faulty conclusions about black consumer behavior:

> Black consumers have too often been described as a homogeneous, undifferentiated market segment consisting of low-income consumers who possess a common set of buying needs. . . . The fact that a high percentage of blacks are below or near the poverty level sometimes leads marketers to assume that all blacks share an equal behavior. This assumption, of course, is false.[16]

Despite the common bond of ethnicity, African Americans are a diverse population. Disparities exist regionally, socially, and economically. Young African Americans, those who did not experience the civil rights movement of the 1960s, are often dramatically different from their parents and grandparents in terms of purchasing habits and consumption patterns.

Upper-income black consumers are likely to purchase items that reflect their status, such as luxury cars and stylish clothing. Limited disposable income does not predict the behavior of black consumers at the lower end of the socioeconomic scale. It has been shown that many poorer black consumers will spend money on high-priced athletic shoes and compact discs.

A national study conducted in 1991, entitled "Market Opportunities in Retail: Insight into Black American Consumers' Buying Habits," revealed the following about African American shoppers:

1. Fifty percent of black consumers do not have a department store preference.
2. Black consumers make up 19 percent of the total health and beauty aids market and 34 percent of the hair care products market.
3. Black consumers are 22 percent more likely to cite shopping as a favorite activity than whites, and 50 percent said they spent their leisure time shopping.
4. More black consumers plan to make a major purchase in the next year than whites. This includes items like cars, stereo equipment, jewelry, and televisions.[17]

Research into African American media behavior indicates that they tend to use the radio more than whites, especially on nights and weekends, and the average African American household views 71.1 hours of weekly televison—higher than any other group. Blacks also prefer magazines more than whites, Asians, or Hispanics. Black local newspaper readership tends to be low, but a higher proportion of blacks than whites reads *USA Today*.[18]

African Americans are heavy consumers of orange juice, soft drinks, compact discs, and cigarettes. They account for 20 to 25 percent of all domestic beer sales, 15 percent of all cola sales, and 9 percent of all domestic car sales. Black women spend 6.5 percent of the family income on clothing, compared with 5 percent of the white population.[19]

African Americans made significant educational gains from 1960 to the mid-1970s, but by the beginning of the 1980s, the numbers of African Americans attending college began to decline. However, in terms of high school graduation rates, an equal percentage of black students earn diplomas as white students.[20]

Half of the 25 million black Americans are female homemakers. They are likely to live in larger households than whites: Half a million live in homes with three or more people, and 28 percent live in households of five or more. The larger households make more trips to the grocery store. The average black family spends almost $3,000 per year on food. The total population spends an estimated $30 billion per year on food.[21]

Black Americans tend to own automobiles: Sixty-seven percent own one or two cars; 30 percent own two or more cars; and 8 percent own a luxury car. They also tend to have bank accounts, own securities, and use credit cards. Eight million of all black Americans have checking accounts. Thirty percent of employed African Americans hold white-collar jobs.[22]

It has been reported that 25 percent of all black college-aged men are in prison, pulling them out of the family and the marketplace.

African Americans are most likely to live in the South and to reside in urban centers like New York, Chicago, Houston, and Philadelphia. Sixty percent of blacks live in the South; 15 percent in the Midwest; 15 percent in the Northeast; and 8 percent in the West.[23]

The demographics indicate that the black middle class has grown over the past 20 years. Simultaneously, there has been an increase in the size of the African American underclass. In other words, there is a growing rift between the "haves" and "have nots."

Because of these differences, there is no guaranteed technique for reaching and appealing to black consumers. However, recent research has uncovered some information marketers might find helpful in communicating with this audience. Research into black consumer behavior has found that African Americans respond differently to advertising than whites. The publisher of Chicago-based *Target Market News* explained black buying decisions this way:

Blacks have a different purchasing dynamic than whites. The factors that go into the black community's purchasing decisions tend to be more traditionally culturally and emotionally based than whites. These patterns seem to be tied to a black person's value system.[24]

The research firm of P. Hunter and Associates found that four major differences can be identified between how African Americans and whites respond to advertising. They include the following:

1. African Americans take advertisements more literally than their white counterparts. African Americans tend to like copy and visuals that directly correspond to one another.
2. African Americans prefer lifestyles and contextual appeals. They find ads more believable that feature people in real situations. They are less responsive to talking heads or single-spokesperson appeals.
3. African Americans tend to prefer ads that represent a variety of cultures—ads that feature people of various hair types, skins tones, and personalities.
4. African Americans look for positive images of black life.[25]

➤ Profile of the Hispanic Market

While the United States was experiencing economic prosperity during the 1980s and the advertising industry was responding to cries of sexism and clutter, a demographic phenomenon was occurring: The Hispanic population was growing at an unprecedented pace. As early as 1981, news reporter Kitty Dawson called the Hispanic market a "missed opportunity."[26]

In 1950, the Hispanic population was 4 million. It grew to 6.9 million in 1960; 9 million in 1970; and 14.6 million in 1980. Between 1980 and 1990, the Hispanic population in the United States grew 67.7 percent, from 14 million to nearly 25 million, according to the U.S. Bureau of the Census.[27] This number represents 10 percent of the total U.S. population. Many believe these numbers are conservative because they do not include "undocumented" Hispanics who cross the border illegally, but who hold jobs and spend money on American goods and services. It is estimated that 46.2 percent of all Hispanics who immigrate to the United States do so without documentation.[28] The population also experiences a high birth rate. Thirty-seven percent more Hispanics are born each year than die.[29]

The Census Bureau uses four categories to segment Hispanic Americans. Mexican Americans make up 60 percent of the Hispanic population and tend to reside in the Southwest and West. They are most heavily concentrated in

California and Texas.[30] Puerto Ricans are the second largest group, with an estimated 2.6 million people, many living in New York City. More than 1.7 million Hispanics come from Central and South America, and another million are identified as Cubans, who are most heavily concentrated in South Florida. A category known as "other Hispanics" totals 1.4 million.[31]

More than three-fourths, or 76 percent, of all U.S. Hispanics reside in just five states: California, Texas, Illinois, New York, and Florida. Within these states, Hispanics are most likely to reside in major metropolitan areas. Nine out of 10 Hispanic Americans live in the nation's 10 top ADIs (areas of dominant influence).[32] Los Angeles has the largest number and highest concentration of Hispanics, with 5.3 million people representing 33 percent of the area's total population. New York is second, followed by Miami and San Francisco.[33]

The Hispanic population is predominantly young. The median age of American Hispanics is 24, six years younger than the overall population. Cubans are the exception, with a median age of 39.1 in 1987, which is markedly older than the general population.[34]

Hispanic households tend to be larger than those of other segments of the U.S. population, which means they are likely to buy more products more often, purchase larger quantities, and visit stores with greater frequency than others. On average, Hispanics spend $107 per week for groceries, as opposed to $90 per week among non-Hispanic shoppers.[35]

Hispanics present a tough marketing challenge, often requiring narrow and precise segmentation. Several major marketers, including Campbell's Soup, American Express, and Domino's Pizza, have launched Spanish-language campaigns with some success. Charles Morrison, a vice president of Coca-Cola, told the *Wall Street Journal*, "Anybody who looks at the size of the Hispanic consumer segment would have to be nuts not to do business there."[36] In the same article, Liz Castells, product manager for Campbell's Hispanic food division, said, "It's a population whose importance can't be denied any longer."[37]

Other companies have jumped on the bandwagon. Pillsbury, Domino's Pizza, Procter & Gamble, and Kraft Foods have all sponsored major efforts to reach the Hispanic market. Coca-Cola hired major league baseball pitcher Fernando Valenzuela as a spokesperson. Coca-Cola's major competitor, Pepsi, whose marketing strategy favors younger consumers, used pop singer Gloria Estefan and the Miami Sound Machine to promote the brand. The Burrell Agency urged Procter & Gamble to select Hispanic fashion designer Ofelia Montejano as a spokesperson for Gain detergent.

The Hispanic market is difficult to crack because although it is large, it is highly concentrated geographically. According to the *Wall Street Journal*, the largest markets in terms of money spent on Hispanic advertising are Los Angeles, Miami, New York, and Chicago.[38] The heavy concentration of Hispanics in a few major markets makes national advertising an inefficient proposition. Furthermore, within the Hispanic market there are distinct sub-cultures with different attitudes, lifestyles, and consumer interests. A close examination of the diversity of the marketplace provides some indication as to why segments of the Hispanic market respond differently to advertisements aimed at reaching them.

At the end of the 1980s, the median family income for Cubans was $27,500, or 65 percent higher than that of Puerto Ricans, who are the most likely Hispanics to live in poverty.[39] Cubans were also employed in 22 percent of all the managerial positions and professional jobs held by Hispanics, as compared with 10.9 percent for Mexicans and 13.5 percent for Puerto Ricans. More than 25 percent of the Mexican Americans employed are categorized as laborers; 17 percent of Cubans fit that label.[40] These clear-cut disparities in income and occupations within the Hispanic population translate into different consumption and lifestyle patterns, which make wide-reaching advertising campaigns wasteful, at best.

Even the choice of a language to use in an ad campaign aimed at Hispanics can be a tricky decision. Less than half of the population (43 percent), or about 10 million people, say they speak English fluently.[41] Over three-fourths (83 percent) speak Spanish at home, the place where they receive much of their advertising information. Even less say they read English fluently. Younger and more affluent Hispanics prefer to speak English, whereas older members of the market prefer Spanish.[42]

The cultural influences of Hispanics migrating from different countries and residing in different regions also need to be considered. Hispanics from the Caribbean are more likely to respond to ads reflecting older, more traditional values. Campbell's Soup used a grandmother figure in its product aimed at Hispanics from the Caribbean, in contrast to the younger models and up-tempo music it features in its Mexican American ads.

Other lifestyle considerations include median age and size of Hispanic families. While baby boomers are getting older, the Hispanic population is getting younger.

Family size varies within the Hispanic population. The largest families are in the largest group, that is, Mexican Americans, with an average of 3.8 members. The national average is 2.7. Cubans have the smallest families with 3.1 persons; Puerto Ricans are in the middle at 3.5 persons per household.[43]

Unemployment among Hispanics is generally higher than for whites, but consistently lower than African American joblessness.

Research indicates that Hispanics are brand loyal and brand looking. Brand loyalty is thought to be a function of family dynamics; that is, Hispanic shoppers want to please the members of their households. Perceived quality, consistency, and tradition are also believed to influence the brand-loyal behavior of Hispanic consumers.[44]

The concept of "brand looking" refers to the Hispanic consumers' need to learn as much as they can about the products they use, according to Carlos

Rossi, president and CEO of Conill Advertising in New York. Hispanic shoppers tend to be familiar with only a few brands but want updated information about these products.[45]

Research has helped marketers to become more sophisticated since the 1970s, when General Motors attempted to sell the Chevy Nova in Mexico without realizing that "Nova" translated into "no go." But the strategies employed by marketers to reach Hispanic audiences still often miss the mark.

One popular technique of the early 1980s was to replace white models with Hispanic models and translate English into Spanish. Such advertising strategies make faulty assumptions about the Hispanic audience. For example, an effort to sell a product like fabric softener to a Hispanic woman who recently migrated to the United States is ineffective if she doesn't understand the concept of two-step laundry—wash first and then soften.

Problems of discovering just how much the Hispanic market understands about American products spawned Market Development, Inc. (MDI) in 1978. The company helps Fortune 500 firms with Hispanic market strategy development. Market Development also created the Hispanic Copy Test, the first foreign-language copy test designed in the United States.[46]

Merely translating English advertising copy into Spanish can result in sending the wrong message or no message at all. As is the case for other ethnic groups, presumptions about the attitudes and cultural values of Hispanics can lead to marketing fiascoes like the Frito Bandito campaign discussed earlier.

The Hispanic market has been called the darling of the industry. The growth in advertising and media outlet expenditures tends to indicate that this is true. One of the reasons Hispanic advertising expenditures have grown so rapidly is because there are outlets designed to reach the Hispanic population. More than any other ethnic group in America, Hispanics have an impressive media system, an avenue through which the target audience can be reached effectively and efficiently.

Hispanic media advertising expenditures doubled between 1983 and 1988.[47] Approximately $550 million was spent in 1988, much of it (45.8 percent) in Spanish-language television, the fastest-growing segment of the television industry.[48] Major marketers like Hallmark and First Chicago Corporation joined forces to purchase Spanish-language television stations for between $300 and $500 million.[49]

The second largest advertising expenditures were for national and local radio (33 percent). There are Spanish radio stations in New York, Chicago, Fresno, El Paso, and Miami. Ad expenditures were lowest for print media at 9 percent.[50]

Spanish International Network (SIN) boasts 241 affiliates, 121 full-time cable stations and 120 full-time Spanish-language radio stations. It also owns numerous print outlets. Over 50 new advertisers joined the network in 1987, including General Motors and Wendy's.[51] UniVision, the first Spanish television network, began operating in 1961 and now owns 13 stations in major markets such as Miami, Fresno, San Francisco, and Phoenix.[52]

The growth in advertising expenditures reflects the media consumption patterns of Hispanics. It is reported that 70 percent of Hispanics listen to radio for entertainment. About 30 percent read five or more magazines, compared with 39 percent of whites. About 29 percent read four or more newspapers. Research has also found that Hispanics watch less television than blacks, but more than whites.[53]

Magazine readership of Hispanics leans toward sports and scientific publications. They tend to prefer their own media to general market media, a trend that is most noticeable in older and less acculturated members of the group.[54]

Writer Jacqueline Sanchez suggests that advertisers follow eight guidelines in trying to reach Hispanic audiences. These include the following:

1. Give detailed product information; use product demonstrations.
2. Stick to literalism and reality; use strong visual images.
3. Use testimonials. Hispanic consumers are less skeptical than others about testimonials.
4. Show a colorful, upbeat environment.
5. Understand that pleasing the family is important to Hispanics.
6. Go for neutrality in accent, appearance, and lifestyle.
7. Use informal Spanish in a Spanish-language ad.
8. Stay away from translated or dubbed commercials; translations don't always work.[55]

These guideposts are not written in stone, but they do provide some insight into which techniques to use and which to avoid in reaching the influential Hispanic market.

The Asian American Market

Asian Americans have been called the "model minority," whose frugality, honesty, and entrepreneurial spirit have made them prosperous, affluent, and powerful. As early as 1984, *U.S. News & World Report* called Asian Americans a group to be reckoned with. Despite their rapid growth, Asian Americans represent less than 5 percent of the total U.S. population.[56]

Like Hispanic Americans, Asian Americans are not a single race of people: Categories include Chinese, Japanese, Koreans, Pacific Islanders, Filipinos, and Vietnamese.

成家立室，保障幸福家庭。
[大都會]與您是天作之合！

　尋找到理想的終身伴侶，共同創造幸福家庭，是人生歷程的一個新開始。要確保新生活的美滿和幸福，夫婦倆人除了要同心努力，更要為未來作出計劃。
　信譽優良，實力雄厚的大都會保險公司是您們計劃幸福家庭的最佳伙伴。大都會管理資產超過一千二百億美元，一向了解和關注華人家庭的需求。其包羅萬有的保險、投資服務，是您們創造新生活的天作之合。

大都會保險公司, 使您高枕無憂

Courtesy L³ Advertising.

It is projected that by the year 2000, there will be 9.8 million Asian Americans in the United States.[57] Chinese and Filipinos will be the largest groups in the nation. Filipinos are expected to represent 21 percent of the total Asian American population, while U.S. Chinese will make up 17 percent.[58] Sixteen percent will be of Vietnamese descent, and 10 percent will be Asian Indian. Nine percent of the Asian American population will consist of Japanese; 14 percent will be categorized as "other."[59]

Like Hispanics, Asian American households are larger than those of other Americans. There is generally more than one worker in the home, resulting in higher household incomes. Also like the Hispanic population, Asian Americans tend to live in urban areas. Of these, 56 percent live in California and Hawaii.[60]

Their economic clout rests in their educational and income levels. Asian Americans are the fastest-growing minority group on college campuses. About 33 percent of all Asian American adults hold college degrees, compared with 16 percent of white Americans. Ninety-six percent of all Japanese males complete high school; 94 percent of Koreans earn a high school diploma.[61]

The 5 million Asian Americans in this country spend an estimated $35 billion annually.[62] They are the only ethnic group with a higher median income and lower unemployment than whites. They also save 20 percent of everything they earn, a rate considerably higher than the national average.

Asian Americans have been called a marketer's dream. Whether they become a marketer's reality has yet to be proved. To close the gap between dream and reality, markets need to understand some salient factors. First, Asian Americans are highly concentrated in only a few states, including California, Hawaii, New York, Illinois, Texas, and New Jersey.[63] Second, Asian Americans are distinct among minorities in terms of their media and consumer buying patterns. Media usage tends to mirror that of whites rather than that of other minority segments. They listen to less radio than Hispanics, use more newspapers as information sources than either African Americans or Hispanics, and prefer to read business-related magazines.[64] Television was cited as the most influential advertising medium, followed by newspaper, magazine, radio, billboard, theater, and flyers. Because of the Asian population's interest in business and technology, marketers tend to target them with financial services and electronic products.[65]

L[3] Advertising Agency in New York conducted consumer behavior research on New York Asians. The agency found that in Asian American households, purchasing decisions are often made by both husband and wife. Wives alone make few major purchasing decisions.[66] The research also indicated that this target audience receives product information from a variety of sources. Word of mouth is important among the Asian population. Eighty-five percent of the respondents said a friend's recommendation was their primary source of product information. Advertising was second at 48 percent, followed by past experience with the product (38 percent) and by *Consumer Reports* magazine (24 percent).[67]

Though many Asians are not as brand loyal as Hispanics, they are brand aware. The L[3] research indicates that product categories in which a brand name is important includes automobiles, major appliances, audio equipment, cameras, video equipment, and fragrances. Respondents in the study were five times more likely to name "Porsche" than "Chevrolet" as the first automobile brand name that came to mind.[68]

A commonality between the Asian and Hispanic markets is a strong tie to family and culture. However, there is a difference in how these values are expressed. Asians tend to celebrate less frequently than Hispanics, and are less likely than other segments of the population to entertain guests in their homes or in restaurants.

In summary, the Asian population in America is growing rapidly, even though the actual numbers are small. Because of the diversity of the group, marketers cannot aim messages to all Asian Americans at one time. However, there are some similarities within the population that marketers can address.

1. Asian Americans have strong ties to family and culture.
2. Older Asians like to see advertising in their native language.
3. Newspapers are a powerful medium for reaching Asian Americans.
4. Asian Americans have a strong need to please and impress their families through the products they purchase.

The Native American Market

Native Americans are the poorest of all ethnic minorities. Nearly 30 percent live below the poverty line as compared with 13 percent for the general population. The unemployment figure among Native Americans holds steady at about 35 percent.[69] Their median income is $10,000 less than the national average.[70]

Few marketing efforts are aimed at Native Americans because their numbers are so small and because the group tends to be isolated. Products aimed specifically at Native Americans are similar to those targeted to other ethnic groups, such as liquor.

Advertisers have used Native American symbolism in messages aimed at other audiences. Chrysler named one of its rugged products the "Jeep Cherokee." An Indian woman graces products made by Land O Lakes. These images are most often used to convey messages about the product and its consumers, rather than to sell to Native Americans.

When and if marketers decide to aggressively approach the Native American market, they might consider using radio to deliver their message. Native Americans have their own media outlets, including radio stations and newspapers. There are approximately 18 noncommercial and 4 commercial Native-owned radio stations in the United States. Many operate in Native languages.[71]

The prosperity of Native Americans is expected to increase as the group gains more education. More than two-thirds (66 percent) of Native Americans now graduate from high school, which is an increase of 11 percent over 1983 figures.[72] Tribes have begun to investigate and develop their own businesses, from gambling casinos to shopping malls. They are learning to use their land as economic clout. As they create businesses, they create jobs for their people. If the trend toward better economic and educational conditions continues for Native Americans, marketers will surely find them in their search for new consumers.

Barriers to Researching Ethnic Markets

For all that is known about ethnic audiences, much remains a mystery. Marketers have conducted limited research aimed at uncovering nuances of these consumers. There is still plenty of guesswork, speculation, and conjecture surrounding ethnic groups, what they buy, how they live, and how messages affect them.

Some researchers have avoided black consumers because of the perception that they are difficult to reach, unapproachable, and uncooperative. Language differences have prevented investigators from questioning the Asian and Hispanic markets. Size, or lack of, is the reason most often given for not conducting research on the Native American consumer. Although all of these reasons might have merit, they are not good excuses for ignoring these markets. Traditional research methods need to be abandoned, and new ways of locating subjects, asking questions, and analyzing answers must be created.

Some ethnic advertising executives recommend face-to-face research in community centers, using ethnic investigators to ask questions and asking questions in a manner that has relevance for the subject. Ken Smikle, publisher of *Target Market News*, a publication that covers marketing to minorities, said it takes commitment on the part of top management to make researching ethnic groups a reality. He suggested that without such support, real information about ethnic consumers will remain elusive.[73]

DISCUSSION QUESTIONS ◄-----------------------------

1. If you were designing a research project for a cosmetic company aimed at uncovering information about consumer behavior patterns of female Hispanic immigrants, what questions would you ask?
2. Is it necessary to be of a specific ethnic background to gather information about members of the group?
3. Other than its size, what other reasons might prevent marketers from pursuing the Native American population?
4. If the Asian market is so affluent, why haven't more advertisers reached out to it?

Endnotes

1. "The African American Market: Community, Growth and Change," *Sales and Marketing Management* 143, no. 3 (May 1991): 25–26.
2. *1994 U.S. Hispanic Market Study* (Miami: Strategy Research Corporation, 1994), 1.
3. "Successful Marketing to U.S. Hispanics and Asians: Players, Agencies and Media," *An American Management Association Research Report on Target Marketing,* American Management Association Publications Division, 1987, New York, 79.
4. John W. Wright, ed., "The American People Today," *The Universal Almanac* (New York: Andrews and McMeel, 1989), 233.
5. Jon Berry, "Help Wanted," *Ad Week* (9 July 1990): 28–31.
6. *1994 U.S. Hispanic Market Study,* 1.
7. Wilton Woods, "American Indians Discover Money Is Power," *Fortune* (19 April 1993): 138.
8. Scott Hume, "Barriers to Data Remain High," *Advertising Age* (1 July 1991): 20.
9. D. Parke Gibson, *The $30 Billion Negro* (New York: Macmillan, 1978).
10. Ken Smikle, telephone interview by Gail Baker Woods, February 4, 1994.
11. U.S. Department of Commerce, Bureau of the Census, *Current Population Reports* (April 1990): P-25-1095.
12. Ibid.
13. "Market Opportunities in Retail: Insight into Black American Consumers' Buying Habits," Deloitte and Touche Trade Retail and Distribution Services Group, New York, January 1991.
14. U.S. Department of Commerce, *Current Population Reports.*
15. "Market Opportunities in Retail."
16. Douglas W. Mellott, Jr., *Fundamentals of Consumer Behavior* (Tulsa: Pennwell Publishing, 1983), 125.
17. "Market Opportunities in Retail."
18. Ibid.
19. Ken Smikle, *The Buying Power of Black America* (Chicago, Ill.: Target Market News Group, 1992).

20. "Market Opportunities in Retail."
21. Smikle, *The Buying Power of Black America*.
22. "Market Opportunities in Retail."
23. U.S. Department of Commerce, *Current Population Reports*.
24. Smikle interview.
25. P. Hunter and Associates, *Report on Black Buying Behavior* (Chicago, 1991).
26. Kitty Dawson, "Advertising's Missed Opportunity: The Hispanic Market," *Marketing and Media Decisions* (January 1981): 68.
27. U.S. Department of Commerce, *Current Population Reports*.
28. U.S. Immigration and Naturalization Service, 1990.
29. U.S. Department of Commerce, *Current Population Reports*.
30. *1994 U.S. Hispanic Market Study,* 12.
31. Alfred J. Jaffee, "New Immigration Act: What's Impact on Population Size?" *Television/Radio Age* (November 1986): A3–A14.
32. U.S. Department of Commerce, *Current Population Reports*.
33. Jaffee, "New Immigration Act."
34. Ibid.
35. *A Closer Look at Conill* (New York: Conill Advertising, Inc., 1993).
36. José de Cordoba, "More Firms Court Hispanic Consumers—But Find Them a Tough Market to Target," *Wall Street Journal* (18 February 1988): Sec. 1, 25.
37. Ibid.
38. Ibid.
39. Ibid.
40. Jaffee, "New Immigration Act."
41. *1991 U.S. Hispanic Market Study* (Miami: Strategy Research Corporation, 1991), 174.
42. *1994 U.S. Hispanic Market Study,* 55.
43. *1991 U.S. Hispanic Market Study,* 161.
44. Joel Saegert, Robert J. Hoover, and Mayre Tharp Hilger, "Characteristics of Mexican American Consumers," *Journal of Consumer Research* 12, no. 1 (June 1985): 104–109.
45. Carlos Rossi, interview by Nileeni Meegawa at Conill Advertising, March 20, 1993.
46. Wally Wood, "Tools of the Trade," *Marketing and Media Decisions* (1986): 154–156.
47. Carlos D. Balkan, "The Hispanic Market's Leading Indicators," *Hispanic Business* (December 1988): 26–28.
48. Ibid.
49. George Swisshelm, "High Station Prices Focus New Spotlight on Spanish Potential," *Television/Radio Age* (November 1986): A15.
50. Balkan, "The Hispanic Market's Leading Indicators."
51. Swisshelm, "High Station Prices," A19.
52. Christy Fisher, "Turmoil in Wake of Univision Sale," *Advertising Age* (8 June 1992): 4.
53. Nejdet Delener and James P. Neelankavil, "Informational Sources and Media Usage: A Comparison Between Asian and Hispanic Subcultures," *Journal of Advertising Research* (June/July 1990): 47.
54. Ibid., 57–58.

55. Jacqueline Sanchez, "Some Approaches Better than Others When Targeting Hispanics," *Marketing News* (25 May 1992): 8.
56. U.S. Department of Commerce, *Current Population Reports.*
57. Robert W. Gardner, Bryant Robey, and Peter C. Smith, "Asian Americans: Growth, Change and Diversity," *Population Bulletin* 40, no. 4 (Washington, D.C.: Population Reference Bureau, Inc., 1985).
58. Ibid.
59. Ibid.
60. U.S. Department of Commerce, *Current Population Reports.*
61. Eric Rolfe Greenberg et al., "Successful Marketing to U.S. Hispanics and Asians," *American Management Association Membership Publications* (New York: 1987), 81.
62. John W. Wright, ed., "The American People Today," *The Universal Almanac* (New York: Andrews and McMeel, 1989), 236–237.
63. U.S. Department of Commerce, *Current Population Reports.*
64. Delener and Neelankavil, "Informational Sources and Media Usage," 45–52.
65. Ibid., 51.
66. Greenberg et al., "Successful Marketing to U.S. Hispanics and Asians," 83.
67. Ibid., 84.
68. Ibid., 89.
69. Wilton Woods, "American Indians Discover Money Is Power," *Fortune* (19 April 1993): 138.
70. Ibid.
71. Bruce L. Smith and Jerry C. Brigham, "Native Radio Broadcasting in North America: An Overview of Systems in the United States and Canada," *Journal of Broadcasting and Electronic Media* (Spring 1992): 183–193.
72. Woods, "American Indians Discover Money Is Power."
73. Smikle interview.

The Legal and Social Environment

4

This chapter reviews governmental legislation of commercial speech and discusses the social environment within which advertising messages are conveyed to ethnic audiences. The controversy surrounding advertising campaigns that target ethnic groups for particular products is also explored. The primary focus is on cigarette and liquor advertising because these two product categories are most often cited as areas for additional governmental regulation, and because cigarettes and liquor are heavily marketed to ethnic audiences.

At the end of this chapter, students should be able to do the following:

1. Understand current legal statutes that influence ethnic advertising
2. Have a working knowledge of the role of industry self-regulation
3. Understand the nature and scope of complaints minorities and others express about advertising aimed at them
4. Be able to identify examples of insensitivity and bad taste in ethnic advertising

➤ The Legal Environment

In 1791, Congress adopted the First Amendment to the Bill of Rights. It states:

> Congress shall make no law abridging the freedom of speech, or of the press, or the right of people peaceably to assemble, and to petition the government for a redress of grievances.[1]

In short, the First Amendment protects free speech. But in 1942, the Supreme Court ruled that the First Amendment did not protect *commercial advertising*, defined as speech that promotes a commercial transaction. The Court stated that advertising did not serve the First Amendment interest of protecting free discussion that contributes to decision making in a democracy.

Since that time, issues such as how advertising is defined, whom it effects, and how it is regulated have led to lawsuits, court decisions, and consumer advocacy claims. Who can and cannot advertise, to what audiences advertising can be aimed, what products are suitable to promote, and how much and what type of information is contained in an ad are just a few of the issues that have been discussed by the advertising industry and those who regulate it. In fact, regulating advertising is the major focus of a number of federal agencies.

The best known is probably the Federal Trade Commission (FTC), the agency that looks for deception and unfairness in advertising. The Wheeler–Lea Act of 1938 gave the FTC the power to investigate and prosecute those engaged in unfair and deceptive advertising. The agency defines "deceptive" as any ad in which "there is a misrepresentation, omission, or other practice that is likely to mislead the consumer acting reasonably in the circumstances, to the consumer's detriment." The FTC's interpretation of what is "unfair" has not been clarified to the satisfaction of many advertisers. The agency calls unfairness the omission of important information. According to the FTC, advertising is also unfair when consumers are "unjustifiably injured."

When the FTC receives a complaint, it investigates the claim and makes a determination. If the advertisement is found to be unfair or deceptive, the agency can issue a cease-and-desist order, which prohibits the ad from appearing.

The advertiser can be fined up to $10,000 under FTC policy. The FTC can also require an advertiser to spend a proportion of its advertising budget on corrective messages if misleading claims have been found.

Other regulatory agencies are the Food and Drug Administration, with authority over labeling and packaging health and therapeutic products; the Consumer Product Safety Commission, the group that enforces safety standards of products and often issues recall orders; and the Federal Communications Commission (FCC), which is responsible for what is transmitted over the public air waves.

In addition to government policy and legislation, the advertising industry regulates itself through codes, ethics, and standards of behavior. But because these measures are voluntary, they are impossible to enforce. Fairness, accuracy, truth, and sensitivity are often left up to the social consciousness of the advertisers and the agency representing them.

Few products are severely restricted from advertising. In 1970, Congress banned cigarette advertising on radio and television. Despite this move, cigarettes remain heavily advertised. The market was estimated to be worth $43 billion in 1988.[2]

Access to Advertising

Ethnic-owned publications and businesses have complained that they are not given equal access to advertising revenues. This issue prompted Cardiss Collins, an Illinois congresswoman, to introduce legislation in 1986 to help end what she called discriminatory practices in advertising. The Non-Discrimination in Advertising Act aimed to do the following:

1. Deny income tax deductions for advertising expenses of persons who discriminate against minority-owned or formatted broadcast or print media in the purchase or placement of advertisements
2. Allow the IRS to determine on receipt of a complaint of discrimination whether a person has engaged in discriminatory conduct
3. Direct the IRS to disallow deductions for any advertising expense in a taxable year in which a person or entity has engaged in discriminatory practices
4. Permit a party discriminated against to bring civil suits on behalf of himself and others
5. Allow the party discriminated against to recover lost profits, consequential damages, and attorney fees
6. Permit the court to assess treble damages in willful and wanton cases of discrimination[3]

The measure was supported by some groups, like the National Association of Black Owned Broadcasters (NABOB), which believed it would help eliminate inequity in advertising placement. It was denounced by the American Civil Liberties Union (ACLU), which charged that it would curb free speech. The bill was defeated.

The arguments for and against restricting specific advertising messages tend to center on the issue of free speech. The same is true for where and how advertisers spend their money. In a free-market economy, advertisers can send messages to whatever audiences they select through whatever media are appropriate, as long as the media are legal. It is unlikely that new legislation will be enacted that specifically prevents them from doing so.

The Social Environment

A Catholic priest whitewashes billboards on the South Side of Chicago to protest the sale of liquor and cigarettes to black communities. A Native American tribal court judge denounces a liquor company for defaming the name of a great Sioux leader. A major insurance company quietly hires a black advertising agency to help improve its image among black consumers in the middle of a lawsuit over auto insurance rates. A national restaurant chain promises more minority jobs after pickets line up to protest discriminatory service. These are examples of how the social environment in ethnic communities has changed in recent years for advertisers. A company cannot simply select an audience to target without first considering health issues, social concerns, and political ramifications. An advertiser must carefully weigh the benefit of potential profit to be gained from ethnic audiences against the risk of long-term alienation from these financially powerful groups.

The idea of using social pressure against a product marketer to obtain a desired goal is not new. In 1982, the Reverend Jesse L. Jackson led boycotts that produced $62 million from Seven-Up, $30 million from Coca-Cola, and $180 million from Heublein. The money was designated for black advertising agencies, distributors, and jobs.

In 1992, the National Newspaper Publishers Association (NNPA), a group of 200 black newspapers, threatened a boycott against Procter & Gamble (P&G) because it believed the company wasn't buying enough space in its publications. NNPA president Robert Bogle noted that black consumers were particularly loyal to P&G products, but that black newspapers were not getting their fair share of the P&G advertiser dollars. The company disagreed, citing that only 1 percent of its total advertising budget was used in print and that the NNPA papers were receiving a fair proportion of that. The boycott did not produce any significant changes in advertising revenue for the black newspapers.

Although ethnic consumers are still using boycotts as a means for getting the attention of advertisers, the mood in recent years has been more aggressive. Property has been destroyed, and demands that specific products be removed from the shelves have become more vehement. Some ethnic communities have decided that they no longer wish to be on the receiving end of messages from certain marketers. In protest, community activists have targeted billboards, which have always been a dominant feature on the urban landscape. They appear on railroad tracks, near expressways, and on the sides of buildings. Of the $696 million spent on outdoor advertising in 1993, alcohol and tobacco accounted for approximately $163 million or about one-fourth of total spending.[4]

In 1990 Reverend Michael Pfleger, pastor of St. Sabina Catholic Church in Chicago, began painting over messages from alcohol and tobacco companies that appeared in his predominantly black parish. The same was done in New York and Dallas. The activists claimed that advertisers unfairly targeted minority audiences who were most likely to be using unhealthy products.

On the other side of this argument are advertisers and the black media. Advertisers claim that destroying their messages interferes with their right to free speech. They further claim that they voluntarily abide by a policy that limits billboard displays within 500 feet of schools, playgrounds, and churches. Black newspapers and magazines, which are highly dependent on liquor and cigarette ads for their survival, also don't want to see legislation against the sale of these products to black consumers. While the government tries to stop minorities from smoking, the high percentage of smokers in these communities has prompted advertisers and marketers to pursue them aggressively. Black magazines earn more of their revenue from cigarette ads than do similar publications. *Jet* magazine earned 10.6 percent of its revenue from tobacco ads in 1987, compared with an average of 6.1 percent for 166 consumer magazines.[5] In 1990, 7.5 percent of advertising in *Ebony* came from cigarette manufacturers; for *Essence*, it was 9.2 percent.[6]

➤ Protests Against Liquor and Cigarettes

Alcohol-related illness and death are prevalent in the African American community. Cirrhosis of the liver, which is related to alcohol consumption, is 70 percent higher among blacks than among whites.[7] While the life expectancy for the general population rises each year, it continues to fall for black Americans. The drop is attributed to AIDS, homicide, and cigarette- and alcohol-related illnesses.

African Americans who protest the heavy marketing of liquor to their communities have complained about the content of the advertising as well as the volume. Concerns have been raised about the sexual nature of liquor advertising aimed at the black community. Most often the ads show men conquering women after drinking malt liquor. Women often are portrayed as sex objects who are turned on by black male liquor drinkers. The images are of masculinity, sexuality, and power. The complaints about content center around the sexual and stereotypical nature of the messages, that is, black men as studs.

Not all liquor advertising aimed at African Americans is for beer. Black consumers drink half of all the cognac sold in the United States, so advertisements for this high-priced liquor are plentiful.[8] Critics of liquor advertising say that associating expensive liquor with the good life is a deceptive form of advertising. Black consumers who cannot attain the lifestyle shown in the ads can do so vicariously by purchasing a bottle of the brand being marketed.

The Latino community, too, has complained that it is unfairly targeted by companies, despite significant health concerns faced by members of the population. One study found that 41 percent of Mexican American men who died of alcohol-related problems did not live to the age of 50, as compared with 30 percent of whites.[9]

Hispanic activists have found the sexual content in some liquor ads aimed at this audience particularly offensive. One Olde English "800" malt liquor ad used a scantily clad Hispanic woman in a provocative pose on a beach with a tiger. The ad read, in Spanish, "It's the Power." Members of the community objected to this message, saying that it inferred that drinking malt liquor would improve the chance for sexual conquest. Other complaints have come from other segments of the Hispanic community who have protested the use of religious symbols and images in liquor advertising.

Native Americans have also protested liquor advertising directed at them. Leaders of the Native American community were actively opposed to the manufacture and sale of Crazy Horse, a malt liquor introduced by Hornell Brewing Company in 1991. The product was to be one in a series of Wild West drinks distributed by the company. Although Hornell denied that Crazy Horse was marketed to Native Americans, its introduction was marked with controversy. Surgeon General Antonia Novello condemned Hornell Brewing Company for what she called insensitive and malicious marketing.

There were several inherent problems with naming a malt liquor Crazy Horse and offering it to Native Americans. The real Crazy Horse—a spiritual and military leader of the powerful Sioux Nation—was opposed to alcohol consumption among his people because he had seen its ravages. The statistics on alcohol abuse among Native Americans are dramatic enough to warrant some consideration as well. Native American alcoholism rates have been estimated to be as high as 80 to 90 percent of the population in some areas.[10]

Hornell stayed with its decision to introduce the product, but the company decided against selling it in 14 states with high Native American populations. In September of 1992, the U.S. Senate approved legislation to prevent Crazy Horse from being marketed. In 1993, the decision was deemed "unconstitutional" by a federal judge in Brooklyn, thus opening the door for the product to return to the marketplace. Judge Carol Bagley Amon, who presided over the case, said that revoking the label approval Crazy Horse received from the Bureau of Alcohol, Tobacco and Firearms was an infringement of Hornell's First Amendment rights. Despite the protests of the Native American community, the product was placed back on the shelves.

Like alcohol, cigarettes have earned the wrath of ethnic minority communities. Smoking rates among African Americans are high at nearly 40 percent.[11] Smoking is such a serious health problem in African American communities that the Centers for Disease Control published *Pathways to Freedom: Winning the Fight Against Tobacco* in 1992. The booklet was designed to help black Americans stop smoking.[12] Among Hispanics, smoking has become an increasingly difficult social problem. In 1983, 28 percent of Hispanic men and women were smokers. That number rose to 30 percent by 1987.[13]

Billboards advertising tobacco products appear in black communities four to five times as much as in white communities. The Tobacco Institute and cigarette manufacturers have repeatedly denied that their efforts represent a conspiracy against ethnic communities. Instead, they claim that what they are doing is niche marketing. Just as Virginia Slims has always been targeted at women and Marlboro was once positioned as a man's smoke, some brands are being marketed as being right for minority groups.

Not all civic and community leaders agree that advertisers should be prohibited from marketing products to any audience they select. Benjamin Hooks, former executive director of the NAACP, said that such tactics imply that blacks need some guardian angel to protect their best interests.

Companies who market alcohol and cigarettes to ethnic minorities walk a fine line. The products they sell are legal. Many adults within the ethnic communities want to consume them. In addition, the products are profitable. The firms continue to sell them because they make money.

The same companies who sell the socially unpopular products also sponsor programs, concerts, contests, and promotions in ethnic communities. Some use minority distributors, advertising agencies, and media to get their messages across. They provide jobs to distributors, bar owners, and liquor stores. Yet, because of the type of products they market, they receive resistance from some members of the target audience. Whether the economic contributions the liquor manufacturers make to these communities are enough to offset the human suffering resulting from the use of the products they sell is the crux of the debate.

Kent smokes... and that's where it's at.

Courtesy Cullers Advertising.

Ethnic communities will not be able to stop the powerful cigarette and liquor manufacturers by whitewashing billboards or complaining about the content of ads aimed in their direction. The only way to change the manner in which these, or any, products are marketed is to disarm the manufacturers by not spending money on the products they sell.

➤ Ethnic Employment in Advertising

In June of 1992, *Advertising Age* ran an article entitled, "The Ad Industry's Dirty Little Secret." In it, information about the lack of minority representation in the advertising industry was revealed. The article reported that black Americans, who constitute 10.1 percent of the total work force, are 5.2 percent of the advertising industry.[14] It also found that many advertising agencies were unwilling to report the number of minorities on their payrolls. Of those who did respond, Leo Burnett's agency reported 12 to 13 percent minorities, Foote, Cone and Belding came in at 18.2 percent, and Della Famina, McNamee reported that 3 of its 32 managers were black.[15]

At the same time, the American Advertising Federation (AAF) adopted a series of objectives to help increase minority participation in the industry. The recommendations were approved by the AAF Council of Governors and Board of Directors on June 15, 1992. The eight objectives are as follows:

1. AAF should increase the minority representation in each community's advertising industry to more closely mirror the percentile mix of minorities in that market.
2. AAF should enlist support from all AAF student and professional clubs and corporate members to implement programs to correct the imbalance.
3. AAF should establish a Minority Affairs position within AAF to assist the development of AAF's efforts to increase minority representation.
4. AAF should seek to confirm more minorities on the Board of Directors, Council of Governors, and headquarters staff.
5. AAF should provide a recognition/awards program to reward those AAF entities that achieved increased minority representation.
6. AAF should establish norms, standards, and evaluative criteria to measure overall results of program initiatives.
7. AAF member ad clubs should be encouraged to provide financial support for the development of minority programs and provide scholarships for minority students.
8. AAF should provide financial, political, and personnel resources to carry forward these efforts within and outside AAF.[16]

It is clear that minority representation in the advertising industry is not reflective of the total population. Like other major businesses, advertising has been slow to achieve its minority hiring goals. But, unlike other industries, advertising is a business of perceptions, images, and persuasion. Its messages go out to all audiences, and its success or failure depends completely on how the information it creates is received.

Advertising has been credited for improving the quality of life for Americans, boosting the economy, and spurring competition. It has been blamed for debasing the language, creating false expectations, and subliminally making people buy things they do not want. Although advertising probably neither creates nor destroys societies, there is little doubt that it does reflect culture. If advertising is to remain the powerful force it is today, it will need to mirror a society that exists, not one that used to be. Doing so will require the industry to look beyond its present borders for talent and skills. Like it has done for many consumers, the industry will have to persuade itself that quality products come in a variety of packages.

DISCUSSION QUESTIONS ◄-------------------------------

1. Should advertisers of unpopular products in ethnic communities change their approach or change their products?
2. Is the advertisers' responsibility to monitor the health of any particular audience?
3. Can an advertiser be expected to run a demarketing campaign against one of its own products?
4. Are ministers and civic leaders being paternalistic toward minority groups?

Endnotes

1. The Bill of Rights, United States Constitution, First Amendment.
2. Judann Dagnoli, "RJR's Uptown Targets Blacks," *Advertising Age* (18 December 1989): 4.
3. Cardiss Collins, "Let's Bring in New Faces," *Ad Week* (29 September 1986): 24.
4. Riccardo A. Davis, "Competition Ignites Outdoor Spending," *Advertising Age* (11 April 1994): 32.
5. A. Ramirez, "A Cigarette Campaign Under Fire," *New York Times,* 12 January 1991, D1, D4.
6. Ibid.
7. "Marketing Booze to Blacks," *Center for Science in the Public Interest* (Washington, D.C.: Public Interest Video Network, 1990).
8. Ibid.

9. M. Jean Gilbert and Richard Cervantes, "Alcohol Services for Mexican Americans: A Review of Utilization Patterns, Treatment Considerations and Preventive Activities," *Hispanic Journal of Behavioral Sciences* 8, no. 3 (1986): 192.

10. Richard G. Schlaad and Peter T. Shannon, *Drugs, Misuse and Abuse* (Englewood Cliffs, N.J.: Prentice-Hall, 1994), 212.

11. Alfred Marcus and Lori Crane, "Smoking Behavior Among U.S. Latinos: A Preliminary Report," in *Advances in Cancer Control: Epidemiology and Research* (New York: Alan R. Liss, 1984), 145.

12. *Pathways to Freedom: Winning the War Against Tobacco* (Philadelphia: Fox Chase Cancer Center, 1992).

13. Marcus and Crane, "Smoking Behavior."

14. Joseph M. Winski, "The Ad Industry's Dirty Little Secret," *Advertising Age* (15 June 1992): 18.

15. Ibid.

16. American Advertising Federation, in letter sent to author, 8 December 1992.

Case
Studies

New Campaign Dresses Up Old Product

Client: Kraft General Foods
Stove Top Stuffing

Agency: Burrell Communications Group
Chicago

Target: African American women

This case is a classic example of repositioning and rejuvenating a product in the latter stages of maturity or early stages of decline. It looks at how advertising can enhance product visibility and awareness with a new audience. It also discusses the role of research in developing a product marketing strategy and advertising campaign.

At the end of this case, students should be able to do the following:

1. Discuss some of the nuances of the African American consumer market
2. Understand the need for purposeful and well-designed research aimed at a specific audience
3. Analyze the differences between an African American campaign and one aimed at the general market

⮞ Profile of the Company

When Phillip Morris purchased Kraft Foods in 1988 and merged it with General Foods Corporation the next year, the nation's largest food marketer was created.[1] North American retail sales for the division were a staggering $18 billion in 1991.[2] Ten percent of all supermarket sales are of Kraft General Foods (KGF) products. With trusted and popular brands like Parkay/Chiffon, Kraft cheese, Post cereals, Maxwell House coffee, and Kool-Aid, it's easy to see why the company is so successful.

KGF consists of seven distinct operating units that manufacture and market food products in the United States, Canada, Latin America, Europe, and Asia. The company's subsidiaries have more than 143 manufacturing and processing facilities in 20 countries.[3]

The company's operating revenue increased 5.4 percent in 1990, and the volume of goods sold in baked goods, beverages, coffee, cereals, and dinners rose between 1989 and 1990.[4] Despite the recent loss of market share among some brands, KGF remains the industry giant. Its marketing budget for North America in 1992 was estimated at $900 million. The company's unchallenged best-seller is Kraft cheese, with 1992 sales of $2 billion and 46 percent of the market share. Another KGF best-seller is Chiffon margarine, with sales at $275 million in 1992.

As individual firms, both Kraft and General Foods had long and well-established reputations. Many of their brands are mature, possessing strong identities and equities. Kraft and General Foods have produced some of advertising's most memorable campaigns, such as the talking Parkay tub, Kraft "cheese and macaroni," and Maxwell House's "good to the last drop" campaign of the 1960s. Baby boomers grew up with Alpha-Bits cereal and Post Raisin Bran.

With the merger came unprecedented growth for KGF for two consecutive years, averaging 20 percent annually.[5] But as profits began to erode to 15 percent in 1991, the company began to seek out new markets and new opportunities. The merger saved the two companies money, increased purchasing power, and streamlined operating expenses—but it also created some problems for the mega-marketer. Because it was so large, the company could not respond quickly to changes in the marketplace. When a recession hit the U.S. economy, a number of KGF brands were affected.

Some brands have fared better than others under the influence of consumer habits, economic forces, and demographic shifts. For example, in the coffee market, estimated at 1.6 million annually, Maxwell House improved its market share in 1991 to 18 percent, or an increase of $16 million.[6] On the other hand, the company lost sales in its frozen vegetables and margarine categories. One place to expand was in the convenience food market.

Kraft General Foods hired Burrell Advertising to develop a campaign for one of the company's older products—Stove Top Stuffing.

What Kraft General Foods Wanted to Accomplish

Kraft General Foods wanted to penetrate the ethnic market, specifically African Americans, with its 15-year-old product, Stove Top Stuffing. General Foods actually pioneered the product category of stuffing mix as a side dish. Its main competitors in this category are Pepperidge Farm and Kellogg. The product has been a steady, albeit seasonal, performer. Generally aimed at women between the ages of 18 and 54, Stove Top Stuffing has most recently been positioned as an alternative to other side dishes. "Stove Top instead of potatoes" was the tagline the brand used to alert consumers to another side dish option.

Stove Top, like any brand no longer in the growth phase of the product life cycle, was vulnerable to decline. Kraft General Foods sought to increase its market share by tapping into the previously unpenetrated African American market. Its goal was to complement the brand's business by creating new interest in a product already on the shelf, thereby avoiding the cost of developing and introducing a new item. Ancillary goals included increasing the number of African American consumers, adding a new dimension to the product, and developing marketing strategies to move the brand ahead in the target market category.

Secondary goals included increasing the frequency of stuffing use. The product is generally associated with special occasions and colder weather. Kraft General Foods wanted consumers to try the product and incorporate it into their everyday lifestyles.

Burrell Advertising account managers wanted to create a position for the product that took advantage of the lifestyles of African Americans, which translated into associating the product with the way black families live and eat. The agency also wanted to show the product in realistic and positive settings, as opposed to stereotypical portrayals of African American life.

African American families are more likely to be headed by females and to reside in urban rather than suburban areas. Because of tradition, they are resistant to a box stuffing. "The item must be familiar to the taste preferences of African Americans, and then they can be convinced to enjoy a familiar taste again, taking advantage of the convenient nature of the product," said Ron Sampson, director of new business development at Burrell.[7]

➤ Concept/Theme Development

Burrell Advertising approached the Stove Top challenge with a set of general hypotheses, including the following:

1. African Americans are more likely to use the term "dressing" instead of "stuffing." Therefore, many did not consider the brand when selecting side dishes.
2. African Americans prefer a cornbread stuffing to the traditional turkey-based product that was the company's leading seller; black women would have concerns about the taste of the product.
3. African Americans view stuffing as something made at home and from scratch—not out of a box.
4. There is a traditional aspect to stuffing among African Americans, with recipes being handed down from one generation to the next.
5. Traditional African American holiday meals include stuffing and potatoes, so positioning the product as an alternative to potatoes was an ineffective approach with the audience.

To test the validity of its hypotheses, Burrell conducted a series of focus group interviews and taste tests with African American women in the target age group (18–54). The women were invited to taste the product, to discuss the concept of a box stuffing mix, and to talk about if and how such a product would fit into their lifestyles. The agency's basic suspicions were confirmed. The women were resistant to a box stuffing because some feared their children would not eat it. Further, the women expressed concern about "cheating" by serving a product that is usually made from scratch. The focus groups also revealed that the turkey broth base was preferable to the cornbread broth, but the cornbread mix tasted better than the turkey broth.

Differences also emerged between younger and older consumers. The younger women, many whom were employed mothers, found the product's convenience appealing. Older women were more likely either to stick with homemade stuffing or to use Stove Top as the foundation to a semi-homemade product. They might add mushrooms, onions, or other ingredients to enhance the product's flavor.

Based on previous research and focus group results, Burrell developed an advertising concept for the product that incorporated the familiar (that is, cornbread dressing) with the unfamiliar (Stove Top Stuffing).

"Mama's making cornbread dressing tonight."

STOVE TOP Cornbread Stuffing Mix.
The box says stuffing.
The taste says dressing.

©1991 Kraft General Foods Inc.

Courtesy Burrell Communications Group.

Execution

To be successful, the advertising concept would also need to include settings that were easily recognizable to the target audience. The goal was to use situations that African Americans would find comfortable and pleasant. It would be unrealistic to show, for example, a single woman serving a box of Stove Top at a dinner party. The concept would also need to avoid stereotypical situations (for example, an obviously poor mother of five children attempting to stretch the family dinner with a box of stuffing).

Burrell developed a simple theme that addressed all the positive attributes of the product while refuting some of the concerns the focus groups expressed. The themeline selected for print advertising was, "The box says stuffing. The taste says dressing." The visuals accompanying the ads were urban settings, for example, a fenced basketball court. A young black male can be seen rapidly exiting the court, as evidenced by the blur on his raised foot. The ad copy reads, "Mama's making cornbread dressing tonight." The theme was tested for recall and appeal on focus groups composed of representatives of the target market. The group found it likable, realistic, and concise. The ads ran in African American women's and family magazines.

Conclusion

Burrell Advertising employed several basic techniques in positioning Stove Top with the target audience. Primary among these was message simplicity. In one sentence, the advertising copy accomplished several tasks. It immediately identified the target audience—African American mothers and their kids. The ad copy also effectively identified the product as cornbread while simultaneously maintaining the product's name, "dressing."

The second basic technique employed was familiarity. The playground setting is one that is familiar to most inner-city dwellers. The use of the black youth in the visual lets readers know this product is aimed at them.

The third basic strategy used in the ad is a clear demonstration of the product's benefits and attributes. The implication is that it is convenient. The scene was apparently shot around dusk, indicating that the product was being prepared tonight—after school and after work.

DISCUSSION QUESTIONS ◄-----------------------------------

1. How should Burrell Advertising have responded if the focus group studies indicated that women didn't like the taste at all?
2. Could the same theme be translated into radio copy without the benefit of the visuals? If so, how?
3. What might the agency do to reach older, more resistant African American women?
4. If KGF wishes to expand its target audience to include Hispanic Americans, what steps should it take?

Endnotes

1. Julie Liesse and Judann Dagnoli, "Goliath KFG Loses Steam After Merger," *Advertising Age* (27 January 1992): 16–17.
2. Ibid.
3. "Kraft General Foods Inc.," *International Directory of Company Histories*, vol. 1 (Chicago: St. James Press, 1988), 530–534.
4. Liesse and Dagnoli, "Goliath KFG Loses Steam After Merger."
5. Ibid.
6. Ibid.
7. Ron Sampson, interview by Gail Baker Woods, at Burrell Communications, Chicago, March 12, 1992.

VIEW FROM THE TOP

Tom Burrell ◄-----------------------------------
Chairman
Burrell Communications Group

Tom Burrell is among the world's foremost experts on ethnic advertising. Since he founded Burrell Advertising in 1971, the award-winning company has grown to rank among the top multimillion dollar agencies in the nation.

   Burrell launched his advertising career in 1960 as a copywriter. Over the next 10 years, the Roosevelt University English major was recruited by several leading ad agencies for his creative approach to the African American consumer market.

He is an active leader in the advertising industry and has made an indelible imprint on attitudes toward and within the African American community.

Burrell has served as the chairman of the Chicago Council of the American Association of Advertising Agencies (4 As), served on the National Advertising Review Board, and has delivered congressional testimony on major issues challenging the industry.

In 1986, the Advertising Club of Chicago awarded him "Advertising Person of the Year" honors and presented him with the Albert Lasker Award for lifetime achievement in advertising. In 1990, Burrell was a recipient of the Missouri Honor Medal for Distinguished Service in Journalism from the University of Missouri.

In addition, Burrell has served on the Chicago Urban League Board of Directors and on its Business Advisory Council, as well as on the Board of Governors, Chicago Lighthouse for the Blind.

Is there a need for ethnic advertising?

Absolutely! Especially for the black market. Black people are not dark-skinned white people. We are different enough and a large enough group to require special and separate efforts. Hence, to tap into this lucrative market, the approach must be much different. Additionally, we are a totally unique group of people in the history of America as a result of having come to the United States in a different manner than others. Our mindset, motivations, and behaviors are grounded in this fact.

But African American people today don't remember slavery. How does an experience that ended more than 100 years ago affect buying habits today?

The less than humane treatment of black people in this country for centuries led to cultural differences in the marketplace that we still see today. Black people's motivation for buying a product is different from that of others. We shop more frequently because traditionally we had less money. We bought smaller quantities because we had less space for storage. We were told that we were inferior—dirty—so we purchased more cleaning supplies. Those subconscious traditions remain today.

Research has shown that African American food purchase patterns differ from the mainstream. Is that true?

For economic reasons, black people were forced to eat chitterlings, greens, and grits. They were inexpensive products that could be stretched to feed a large family. Many of these products remain popular in the black community.

With the understanding that these underlying differences exist in the black consumer, what approach does Burrell take to appeal to this market?

Our approach is one of realism. We show black life as it is—not as a carbon copy of white life. For example, in one of our McDonald's commercials we showed a single mother whose son apparently didn't like his mother's date. The three of them dined at McDonald's. It was an experience they could all share. Other realities of black life include extended families and fathers working two jobs. Wherever appropriate, we employ these themes in our advertising strategies.

Do ethnic agencies have to be particularly socially responsible?

Our advertising agency, like all others, is in the business of increasing sales and market share for our clients. In the process of doing our job we send out positive messages about our clients. It just so happens that the things that sell also enhance the community and help to reinforce a positive self-image. These are fortuitous outcomes of the type of advertising Burrell produces. However, we also make contributions to literary programs, dance theaters, museums, and other community activities. We can support our community because we are doing an effective job for our clients.

Is there a product category you won't sell?

I won't accept cigarette advertising. But what is ethical and unethical is a matter of personal taste. My guidelines are simple. I ask myself what is moral and legal and how my kids would feel about me selling a particular product. If I couldn't tell them for whatever reason, I wouldn't sell the product. I also ask myself if I would want to see my kids use a product that I was selling. Other people have other rules. I once had a partner who didn't want to accept Navy ads because he didn't think it was a good idea for blacks to enter the military. Each agency has to make those decisions for itself.

Advertising is such a competitive business. Is there any danger of the major general market agencies gobbling up smaller, ethnic agencies like mainstream newspapers have disseminated the black press?

When I began my advertising career, the mainstream agencies said there was no such thing as the black market. Obviously, that viewpoint has changed. By recognizing the need for special marketing to ethnic audiences, the mainstream agencies have, in fact, made the area more viable—more sophisticated. That opens up new opportunities for agencies like mine. It is important to understand that black agencies, or any other special market agency, will not survive if they are not competitive and if they don't get the job done for clients.

What do you say to those who believe black agencies can sell products only to black clients?

I say they have a fundamental misunderstanding of what ethnic agencies really do—which is to develop advertising for special markets. For us to be successful, we have to understand the particular marketplace, whatever it is. The fact that we have an expertise in ethnic marketing does not mean we cannot tailor campaigns to any audience. In fact, just the opposite is true. To be experts in ethnic advertising, we have to understand the mainstream culture as well. As minorities, we have lived in two worlds, ours and the mainstream's. Our expertise spans beyond ethnic advertising.

What special approach does Burrell bring to clients?

Our agency takes what I call the "Mark Twain" approach to advertising. Mark Twain wrote his adventure stories for two audiences—kids and adults. He understood them both. Each audience got something different out of his stories. The same holds true in advertising. The ads may be designed ostensibly for minority audiences, but their themes can appeal to others as well. The McDonald's Double-Dutch ad, in which we showed young black girls jumping rope, was popular in Europe and Norway.

Any final thoughts?

Students need to understand that mass marketing is dead. Marketing segmentation is the way of the future. Blanket communication is out. Direct marketing, special publications, and targeted messages are in. Agencies that can deal with any segment of the marketplace, geographical, cultural, or social, will survive. The others won't.

Corporate Giant Toots Its Horn to Gain Ethnic Consumers

2

Client: General Motors
Agency: The Mingo Group
          New York
Target: African Americans
          Hispanic Americans

This case looks at how institutional or corporate advertising can be used to send messages to particular audiences. It examines several techniques employed by a company to win back a previously loyal market eroded by foreign competition. Like all institutional campaigns, this effort intentionally avoids references to specific product lines. Instead, it focuses on the tradition and the social responsibility of the company. It is designed to remind consumers that this company has been a part of their communities for a long time and should continue to be a part of their lives.

At the end of this case, students should be able to do the following:

1. Distinguish between institutional and product advertising
2. Understand what factors motivate a company to use corporate image advertising versus product advertising
3. Recognize what can happen when a segment of the population is taken for granted

➤ Profile of the Company

General Motors (GM), the largest of the Big Three U.S. car manufacturers and the world's largest automaker, was well aware of its eroding market share as the 1980s came to a close. Bombarded by Japanese competitors, plagued by perceptions of poor design and quality, and victimized by its own size, GM found that previously loyal consumers, including African Americans and Latinos, were opting for other automobiles.

The company's problems were not confined to the sale of its automobiles. General Motors, which manufactured military vehicles, radar, guided missiles, and telecommunications equipment, was also adversely affected by a downturn in the weapons industry.[1]

General Motors was best known for its automobiles, and by the close of the 1980s, GM was producing no less than 60 different styles and makes of automobiles and trucks. The company's five divisions—Pontiac, Cadillac, Oldsmobile, Chevrolet, and Buick—were often in competition with one another for limited auto sales dollars. Consumers were having problems distinguishing between the lines. Cadillac was able to maintain the most distinctive identity (that is, the upscale automobile). Middle- and upper-class black consumers, once loyal to Cadillac, moved away from the luxury automobile, showing a preference for foreign models instead. Once perceived as a sure sign of personal success and accomplishment for black drivers, Cadillac was pushed aside by the BMW. The "Beemer," as it was affectionately dubbed, became the new source of pride and achievement.[2]

➤ What General Motors Wanted to Accomplish

Research into black consumer attitudes toward automobile purchases showed that blacks were 12 percent more likely to be planning to purchase a new car than the general population was. Research also indicated that black drivers were more likely to purchase cars at the upper end of the spectrum, such as Mercedes and BMW.[3]

Competition for the black consumer dollar did not come only from Europe. Honda, Toyota, Nissan, Mazda, and the other Japanese automakers were also eating away at GM's market share.

According to the Mingo Group, GM wanted to rekindle a positive attitude among black consumers and enhance its image among African American car buyers. The Mingo Group's job was to inform black audiences of the company's commitment to equality. Because GM wanted to create a positive environment in which its product messages could be received, this campaign was to be as much a public relations enterprise as an advertising effort. General Motors wanted to sell its image as a corporation that understands and supports the efforts of a particular community. The company wanted to restore the faith of the black community in its products and services. Realizing the emotional aspects of automobile purchasing among African Americans, GM wanted to make a conscious effort to appeal to African American consumers on a personal level. This was not just a company that sells cars and trucks; this was a company that cared.

This type of advertising, also known as corporate, institutional, or image advertising, does not aim to reach the target audience with a message about a specific product or service. The primary goal of corporate campaigns like this one is to let consumers know that the corporation is more than just a financial entity. It is an institution built, managed, and supported by people.

The Mingo Group had several major objectives in developing this campaign. First, it wanted consumers to be aware that GM understood them, cared about them, and were supportive of them. Second, the advertising agency wanted African Americans to understand that GM wanted and needed their business. It was important for consumers to know that GM had not taken them for granted.

Concept/Theme Development

Previous research contributed to the creative team's understanding of the relationship between black auto purchasers and the corporation. Realizing the need for creating an emotional bond between consumers and the corporation, the Mingo Group created the following slogan for its GM campaign aimed at African American consumers: "At General Motors we never forget who's driving." The theme accomplished a major objective. It subtly recognized the power of the black consumer; that is, it expressed GM's understanding that a corporation's success or failure is contingent on how consumers respond to the company.

The second theme was built on the premise of a long-term relationship between the auto giant and the black community. "Building Tomorrow

Together" was used as the opening headline to each ad. Scholarships, investments, and suppliers were used as ways through which the company had established its foundation in the community. The basic ideas behind all the sub-themes of the campaign were education, respect, and tradition.

➤ Execution

The Mingo Group turned this campaign into a number of print advertisements in black and white and in color. One print ad features a young black man who is attending college on a GM scholarship. The copy says, "GM is investing in his future, and by doing so is investing in the future of the African American community."

Another print ad shows a young black boy, intently studying an automobile. The headline to the body of copy states, "Someday, I'll reinvent the wheel." The copy gives the reader more insight into the boy's thoughts. "Ever since I was a little kid, I was into cars. How they work. How they look. How I would build them." Through copy and visuals, this ad reinforces GM's commitment to people and not just to automobiles. It closes with the tagline, "We never forget who's driving."

In another execution of the same concept, the reader sees an African American businessman apparently explaining tires to a customer. The entrepreneur is identified in the copy as the owner of a Brooklyn tire and auto service center. The man in the ad tells the reader of his commitment to the community—a commitment he shares with General Motors, the company that provided him with money for his business. Here, GM is "tooting its own horn" but using a credible source to do it. The black businessman is demonstrating gratitude, but also is telling the reader that he has accepted the start GM gave him and is using it to provide quality service to his community.

The Mingo Group used this same concept in a print advertisement aimed at the Hispanic community. The man featured in the ad is an immigrant to this country from Argentina. He is now a supplier of machine services to GM. Like the black businessman, he received assistance from the automaker to help make his business a success. The copy headline, "The American dream is alive and well right here in Livonia, Michigan," evokes thoughts of patriotism, fairness, and accomplishment—tried and true concepts few find offensive and many find appealing. For Latino immigrants, the thought of realizing the American dream is important and motivating—it is why most came to the United States. The businessman shown in this ad serves as a role model for the Hispanic community. If he could do it, they too might have a chance. Further, his opportunities in America were enhanced by a major corporation, that is, General Motors.

BUILDING TOMORROW TOGETHER: INVESTMENT

"My philosophy is simple: The customer! The customer! The customer!"

MATTHEW BROWN
Owner
Big Apple Tire & Auto
Service Center
Brooklyn, N.Y.

"On a daily basis, that means service, service, service! My people are trained to listen and then follow through with the best possible work.

But there's more. I believe I have a responsibility to provide employment, be a role model and simply be involved. I believe that the success of any business is bound up in the well-being of the community. By providing seed capital to me through their Specialized Small Business Investment Company (SSBIC) GM has shown that they share that philosophy."

At General Motors, we are committed to building world class cars and trucks and working with the community to build a healthier economic environment in which to market them. Helping entrepreneurs like Matthew Brown start their own business through our Specialized Small Business Investment Company (SSBIC) helps us build both our futures.

Chevrolet Pontiac
Oldsmobile Buick
Cadillac GMC Truck

GM MARK OF EXCELLENCE

GENERAL MOTORS
We never forget who's driving.

© 1992 General Motors Corporation

Courtesy The Mingo Group.

Conclusion

The Mingo Group used its understanding of black and Hispanic consumers to create a campaign aimed directly at the heart of this audience. The agency took full advantage of its knowledge that black consumers are attracted to emotional appeals. Further, the language of the campaign provided readers with a certain amount of empowerment. This major corporation was asking for respect and appreciation from minority communities.

The careful selection of subjects in the ads lends credibility to the campaign. There are the black and Hispanic businessmen—apparently pillars of their communities—showing support for the same company that backed them. Using community leaders allows the campaign to use the two-step flow of communications, that is, sending a message to the masses through influential people.

In summary, the Mingo Group used a variety of approaches to reach minority auto consumers with GM's institutional message. The common thread through the campaign is the positive and uplifting nature of the advertisements. Readers of the ads learn good things about GM, which in theory contributes to an overall favorable attitude toward the company. Product advertising picks up from this point and gives the consumer specific information about the cars and trucks GM makes—just for them.

DISCUSSION QUESTIONS

1. If you were working on the GM account, how would you measure the success of this type of campaign?
2. Can this campaign be considered successful even if auto sales don't rise?
3. If GM assigned you to a brand account, for example, Cadillac, what type of techniques would you use to reach the African American audience?
4. Is it a good idea for GM to use the same technique on both African American and Hispanic American audiences?

Endnotes

1. "General Motors Corporation," *Moody's Handbook of Common Stocks* (New York: Moody's Investors Service, Spring 1993).
2. Penni Crabtree, "Black Consumer Survey Reveals a Buying Power That Bucks Stereotypes," *Memphis Business Journal* 11, no. 8 (5 February 1990): 12.
3. Ibid.

Sam Chisholm
President and Chief Executive Officer
The Mingo Group

Sam Chisholm joined the Mingo Group in 1980 as vice president and management supervisor. He was promoted to senior vice president and director of Client Services in 1984; executive vice president and general manager in 1988; and CEO in 1990. A graduate of Virginia State University with a bachelor of science in business administration and accounting, Chisholm began his advertising career at Benton and Bowles as a media planner. He has also worked for the Marschalk Company, Continental Can Company, and Jack Tinken and Partners. During his career, Chisholm has worked on a variety of accounts, including Coca-Cola Foods division's Minute Maid juices.

The Mingo Group, founded in 1977, reported billings of $66 million in 1990. It is a full-service agency, offering a variety of services to clients including marketing, media, research, public relations, and creative services. The company is located in Manhattan and employs more than 40 professionals. The Mingo Group's list of clients has included Miller Brewing, the National Urban League, General Motors, the U.S. Army, Maybelline, and Toys "R" Us.

In your opinion, what distinguishes a Mingo ad from another agency's work?

I think a key thing is the human connection. We talk a lot about reaching the heart. We really do recognize that being able to distinguish our clients' products from those of its competitors requires being able to recognize the unique selling proposition. That could be "more spicy chicken" or "brighter whites" or an "easier ride." We not only appeal to the head in the strict unique proposition but also deal with the heart. That's what you will see in all the advertising we develop. We believe that to reach the head, you must touch the heart.

What approach do you take with clients?

We recognize that clients are giving us the opportunity to help build their products, and consequently, that helps us build our business. This is not a not-for-profit organization. This is a business, and we are in it to make money.

Our mission is to leverage our roots in ethnic expertise into advertising and marketing and communications to all consumers driven by an ethnic sensibility. We create preemptive and emotional bonds between the consumer and the client. We address the emotional aspect as well as the client's unique selling proposition.

The Mingo Group is known for its research. Do you have an in-house research department?

We don't have a research department, but we have an affiliation with a research organization that we use on a continuous basis. Our research is not strictly qualitative. We ask ourselves very simple things. We don't ask if this message is going to reach African American consumers—we ask if this message is going to reach us. We are probably better known for our opinions than our research.

Where do you gather information for your clients?

From a wide variety of sources. There is secondary and tertiary research available. There is something called "grandmother research," which means asking ourselves or making some clear observations. Advertising is not an exact science. Research can only provide some statistical indication as to where a consumer might be at a particular point in time. We are also interested in the consumers' attitudes, desires, feelings, and wishes about a product. Numbers don't always indicate that. In fact, they can even handcuff you if not used properly.

What appeals to ethnic audiences?

As I said before, we believe that you have to reach into the heart. The emotions are what we want. Minorities are very emotional people. Take a close look at blacks or Hispanics. They tend to be very loving and very warm, and that's what we are all about. Those are the things we pride ourselves in . . . being able to laugh at and with one another.

In your opinion, do African Americans respond to public relations?

Public relations is important. And as a full-service organization, we offer expertise in all aspects of communications. An example of how we use public relations would be Seagram's gin. It sponsors an African American family Black

History Month celebration each year. We commission a black artist to do an interpretation of the African American family on canvas. These pieces are turned into lithographs, and 100 lithographs are created. All are given to the National Urban League, which sells them for $1,000 a piece. It's both a public relations and a community event.

What do you think needs to be in the campaign to sell the product?

We need to deliver on promises. You have to be talking to the consumer, not over and not below. This consumer has been neglected and knows it. In many ways he or she will respond favorably to attention. It's like going out on a date. Sometimes, you say, "Wow." The consumer says, "Yeah, I understand what you're talking about."

How do you analyze a successful campaign?

Whether it moved the needle. Whether you sold the product.

Paper Company Attempts to Clean Up with Hispanic Audiences

3

Client: Scott Paper Company
Agency: Conill Advertising
          New York
Target: Hispanic consumers

his case is a clear demonstration of how important aspects of Hispanic culture (that is, family, color, celebration) are applied to an advertising campaign aimed at this audience. The focus is on how basic elements of effective advertising can be adapted and modified to meet the needs of specific target groups. This case also provides lessons in research, positioning, the development of an advertising character, animation, and humor. It looks at how a simple product can be made more interesting and appealing.

At the end of this case, students should be able to do the following:

1. Understand the importance of language in communicating with ethnic audiences
2. Distinguish Latino advertising from general market campaigns on the basis of content
3. Discuss the use of visuals and words in creating a cultural mood in advertising

➤ Profile of the Company

Scott Paper Company is the world's largest manufacturers of consumer paper products, with 40,000 employees and 1992 sales reported at $5.36 billion.[1] The company sells sanitary tissue products including toilet paper, paper towels, napkins, tablecloths, plates, and plastic flatware.

The Scott Company was founded in 1879 by the Scott brothers, E. Irvin and Clarence, of Philadelphia. They began by manufacturing wrapping paper and paper bags, but moved into the toilet paper business by the end of the century. The notion of toilet paper was new to the nation at this time, and the idea of advertising and marketing such a personal product was unacceptable. Therefore, the Scott brothers sold their product to private dealers, who packaged and marketed it under a variety of brand names. Recognizing the financial viability of toilet paper sales, the Scott Company later decided to market its own products and to advertise them heavily. Legend has it that a school teacher who didn't think it was sanitary to have students share towels created the paper towel. By 1907, Scott had entered the paper towel business.

Over the next two decades, the Scott Paper Company acquired a number of business interests to support its main function. The company purchased mills, timberland, and new machines. The acquisitions of these holdings helped to make Scott the industry giant. The convenience of paper products, combined with a relatively inexpensive price tag, added to consumers' ever-increasing demand for Scott products.

The company's success continued throughout the 1930s despite the economic ravages of the Great Depression, and its prosperity grew during World War II as Scott purchased more timberland and mills. The decade of the 1950s was equally successful for the company, as its market share grew to 38 percent. Kleenex, the company's major competitor at the time, held only an 11 percent share.[2]

Part of Scott's success is attributable to its understanding of niche marketing. The company has always made only a few products and advertised them aggressively. This philosophy has been maintained throughout the company's history. Between 1955 and 1961, the company introduced only two new products. Sanitary napkins and plastic wrap were extensively researched before the company marketed them to the general public.

Scott's stronghold on the paper industry did not go unchallenged. In addition to Kimberly-Clark, makers of Kleenex, other major players entered the field. Among them was Procter & Gamble, whose extensive resources and impressive distribution system made it a fierce competitor. Procter & Gamble introduced the first disposable diaper, an invention that helped eat into Scott's market share. By 1970, there were 11 other toilet paper manufacturers and 7 facial tissue makers.[3] With an increase in competition and slow growth in the paper products market, the Scott Paper Company lost money in the 1970s and was forced to restructure its business, upgrade its facilities, and sell some of its holdings.

The company began to regain some of its profits and market share during the 1980s, mostly because of an aggressive spending program, decreased production costs, and an increase in demand for catalog and magazine paper. In 1987, the company opened Scott Worldwide, which was created to operate in Europe, Latin America, and the Pacific Basin.

What Scott Wanted to Accomplish

The consumer paper products industry was fully mature by the 1970s. There were few new products being introduced and fewer new consumers to use them. Everybody was already using paper towels and bathroom tissue. The only way to increase consumption was to take consumers away from competitors. This saturation forced Scott to move into international markets to maintain, and possibly increase, its market share.

On the national front, however, Scott recognized that one way to improve sales was to pursue previously untapped markets. Ethnic audiences had been virtually ignored by the paper companies, who assumed that the general market campaigns they developed would reach out to all consumers. Scott took a different approach. Instead of just creating advertising messages for everybody and picking up ethnic consumers along the way, the company decided to investigate the viability of the Hispanic market and to take advantage of its size, income, and brand loyalty. Further, growth projections for the market could mean more profits in the future if Scott could establish a toehold with Hispanics.

Research indicated that Hispanic Americans tend to have larger families than other groups, and they have a strong desire to please their families. They also are brand looking before becoming brand loyal.

According to Carlos Rossi, CEO of Conill Advertising, "brand looking" means that Hispanic consumers are seeking information about a product and are willing to listen and try a number of brands before settling on the one that best suits their needs. Many Hispanics are immigrants who have not been exposed to information about products before their arrival to America. Scott wanted to penetrate this market, get them to accept the company's product, and develop a brand loyal following among Hispanic American consumers.

Concept/Theme Development

Conill's assignment was to create an appealing and effective television campaign for Scott napkins. Market research indicated that 67 percent of Hispanic consumers think it is "very important" to be able to tell which products best meet their needs. Only 40 percent of the total population agreed.[4] This finding pointed to a campaign full of information directly relevant to the target audience. Based on research and experience with the Hispanic market, the agency selected several important themes on which to anchor the advertisements.

First, Conill decided to use the crucial and recurring family theme. Hispanic consumers want their families to be happy with the products they use. Hispanic women, the people most likely to be purchasing paper products, are likely to be extremely conscientious about what type of products come into their homes and in contact with their children.

Quality was another marketing consideration. Hispanic consumers do not like to sacrifice quality for value if it is possible to have both. They like to spend their money wisely and get the most benefit out of the products they purchase. Another aspect of Hispanic consumer behavior useful for marketing Scott napkins was the consumers' desire for consistency and minimal risk. They like products that are reliable and safe. Armed with this information, Conill developed the "Miss Napkin" television commercial expressly for Hispanic audiences.

Execution

One of the problems facing the creative team was the development of a 30-second television ad to meet all of the objectives the research indicated were important. They didn't have a lot of time, but they did have plenty of information. In addition, paper napkins are not a very lively or exciting product and thus do not lend themselves easily to the type of advertising most appealing to the target audience. Hispanics tend to like movement, color, and action, none of which are attributes of paper napkins.

Conill responded to these challenges by creating an animated character for Scott napkins. "Miss Napkin" was obviously female (she had long eyelashes and wore lipstick) and had very expressive eyes and a sense of humor—in

Scott Napkin
"Miss Napkin"

Conill Advertising, Inc.

SPSN-1013 30 SECONDS

NAPKIN: Señora, usted no sabe qué difícil es ser una Servilleta Scott
(NAPKIN: Ma'am, you don't know how difficult it is to be a Scott Napkin.)

Somos tan suaves...
(We're so soft...)

...tan absorbentes...
(...so absorbent...)

...y ni hablar de fuertes...
(...and you want to talk strength?)

...ninguna servilleta de papel es más resistente.
(...no paper napkin is stronger.)

Le damos calidad y, ¿acaso somos caras?
(...We give you quality, but are we expensive?)

No.
(No.)

Ponemos tanta calidad a su alcance
(We put so much quality within your reach...)

Y, ¿qué recibimos a cambio?...
(And what do we get in return?...)

...que nos usen...y usen...
(to be used...and used...)

(SIGH) Así es la vida de una Servilleta Scott...dar, dar, y dar...
(Such is the life of a Scott Napkin...give, give, and give...)

Calidad a su alcance

ANNCR: Servilletas Scott. Calidad a su alcance.
(Scott Napkins. Quality you can afford.)

Courtesy Conill Advertising.

short, she had personality. As the "spokesperson" for the product, Miss Napkin had a number of goals to achieve. She would introduce the product, discuss its strengths and benefits, create a mood about the napkins, and call viewers to action. She was designed to grab their attention, win them over with her warmth, and make them laugh.

In one spot Miss Napkin begins by lamenting the life of a Scott paper napkin. She speaks directly to female homemakers. Thus, the ad immediately targets its audience: Women are supposed to look up and take notice. From that point, Miss Napkin gets into the attributes of the product. She discusses its softness, absorbency, strength, and quality. She makes a particularly strong point about the price, emphatically telling the viewer that the product is inexpensive. After making these salient arguments, Miss Napkin returns to her original demeanor as a complainer. She works so hard for the consumer and gets so little in return. The consumer is the winner because she gets low price and quality. The napkin is there to serve her and her family.

The visual aspect of the ad is notable also. Bright colors—lots of yellows, pinks, and blues—are used in the ad. Miss Napkin is white, but her lips are red, her eyebrows are black, and her eyeshadow is blue.

The visuals also play to the family theme. Softness is a product attribute demonstrated through a frame where a mother wipes the face of a child. Absorbency, too, is shown by way of a child who is eating, drinking, and making a mess. Scott napkins are there to help. Strength is indicated by a picture of a slice of celebration cake being served on a Scott napkin. Convenience is conveyed through a picture of a party tray. The ad leaves the consumer with an impression of quality and affordability. Miss Napkin stresses that the consumer can afford to purchase this excellent product.

The entire ad is written and voiced in Spanish as an effort to give the target audience information in the format they like. In 1984, 68 percent of Hispanics questioned said they spoke their native language at home. By 1994, that number had risen to 83 percent.[5]

➤ Conclusion

Using a combination of bright images, brisk and humorous copy, and animation, Conill was able to develop an effective ad for Scott napkins. The agency overcame a number of challenges in this campaign. It was able to work around a dull product by creating an interesting character. Conill was also able to provide a considerable amount of information to brand-looking Hispanic consumers in a short time frame.

The use of humor helped to keep the product in perspective. Napkins, though not a very serious item, are portrayed as important to the family.

Finally, the ad clearly addresses two issues of concern to Hispanic consumers: price and quality. Without calling the product cheap, the ad indicates that they are inexpensive. The entire purpose of this spot is to make female Hispanic consumers who don't use Scott question their decision to use another napkin and to make users feel comfortable with the purchase they have made.

DISCUSSION QUESTIONS

1. Can the Miss Napkin character be adapted and modified for other Scott products aimed at Hispanic audiences? Should it?
2. What other techniques can the paper company use to reinforce the behavior of Hispanic consumers?
3. Are Hispanic audiences any different from the general population in terms of their expectations of advertising?
4. Would this commercial work in English?

Endnotes

1. "Scott Paper Company," *Moody's Handbook of Common Stocks* (New York: Moody's Investors Service, Spring 1993).
2. "Scott Paper Company," *International Directory of Company Histories*, vol. 1 (Chicago: St. James Press, 1988), 329–331.
3. Ibid.
4. *A Closer Look at Conill* (New York: Conill Advertising, Inc., 1993).
5. *1994 U.S. Hispanic Market Study* (Miami: Strategy Research Corporation, 1994), 55.

VIEW FROM THE TOP

Carlos Rossi
Chairman/ Chief Executive Officer
Conill Advertising

Carlos Rossi has over 20 years of management and marketing experience in the United States and Latin America. He served as brand manager at Procter & Gamble Paper Products and Detergent Division in Puerto Rico and in Cincinnati. He also worked for the Pfizer Corporation and was vice president of marketing for Citibank Caribbean Operations, president of Seagram's Marketing Operations Rum Products, and a senior partner of the Management Shop, a marketing consulting firm. Rossi is a graduate of Indiana University with a degree in political science.

The Conill agency has represented a wide range of clients, including Helene Curtis, Seiko Time Corporation, Land O Lakes, Citibank/Citicorp, Procter & Gamble, and Scott Paper. The company is headquartered in New York and has a full-service office in Los Angeles. Its staff of over 50 represents at least 10 Latin American companies.

Is Conill one of the first Hispanic advertising agencies?

We are the oldest agency advertising to a Hispanic audience. We began in 1968 as a creative boutique founded by two immigrants from Cuba, Mr. and Mrs. Raphael Conill. We bought the agency in 1987 as part of the British conglomerate Saatchi and Saatchi.

What is special about your agency?

We build brands and brand equity. One of the issues for marketing in this country is the assumption that the Hispanic community is like any other minority group. There is no melting pot. Here, you are dealing with a lot of foreign-born people, and you have to treat them as foreigners. You have to build the brands marketed specifically to this community. Let me also say that we are strong believers in accountability. We place considerable responsibility on our research capabilities to help direct and monitor results and efforts.

With such a diverse population, how do you segment the Hispanic community?

Although there are many countries, there is only one language—Spanish. There are many colloquialisms. We look for the similarities, and there are quite a few. We then target the similarities. In Latin America, the general market is Mexican. There may be blond and blue-eyed Mexicans in ads in Mexico. Here in the United States they are not a majority, so a blond, blue-eyed model will not be appropriate to the target audience here.

What does the Hispanic marketplace want from advertisers?

Most Hispanics are new arrivals to this country. They have strong ties to their culture and are hungry for information in Spanish. They need and look for basic information more than general market consumers do.

Research indicates that Hispanics are very brand loyal. Have you found this to be true?

The real truth is that Hispanics are "brand looking." They look for a quality brand and then stay with it. They may pay a slightly premium price if the product is going to serve the purpose well. Where they come from there may be one or two brands in a specific product category. Here, they are faced with much more than that, and they will attempt to try the products. Lying to this consumer in the form of an overpromise can ruin your brand. Word of mouth spreads very quickly in this market.

What other nuances about the Hispanic marketplace have you found in your experience?

It is important to understand that the product represents the individual and the individual's lifestyle—what the person eats, wears, and drives. It is a bad idea to attack a competitive product. Consumers believe that they can make their own decisions, and they consider an attack ad as a failed approach to sell the brand. Competitive ads are okay as long as nothing negative is said about the competitor.

Can you give an example?

Let's say you are advertising Cottonelle bathroom tissue. You can say, "If you like Charmin, you'll love Cottonelle." After establishing the standard of my brand, then I can move the competitive brand aside. If the competition ad attacks the competitive product, consumers will perceive the message as saying they are dumb. This will never appeal to them.

What are the most effective means of reaching the Hispanic audience?

There is greater recall in reaching the Hispanic consumer with a Spanish commercial than with an English commercial. Speaking Spanish at home is increasing. It's in fashion. There are some cities where you can live very comfortably and not need to speak a single word of English.

What services do clients get from Conill that are not available at any general market agency?

We live and breathe Hispanic research, which is critical for design and analysis of a campaign. We know the suppliers and the services they offer. We stay abreast of innovations and improvements in Hispanic measurement. We are aware of areas for potential pitfalls. We understand the importance of promotions, research, expert media placement, and a strong creative approach in building brands. In our opinion, brand-building creative strategy will have five elements: (b)rand's positioning, (u)niversality, (i)nformation, (l)ifestyle relevancy, and (d)imensionalization of one promise or benefit.

How does your agency promote itself?

We do this through reputation and word of mouth from our present clients. Between noncompeting clients they will openly discuss success with an agency. We have obtained a number of clients that way.

What is the biggest problem in Hispanic advertising?

There are not enough qualified people to work in the industry.

Company Seeks Asian Consumers to Insure Continued Growth

Client: Metropolitan Life
Agency: L³
New York
Target: Asian Americans in New York

Over a five-year period, the Metropolitan Life Insurance Company increased its advertising spending aimed at Asian Americans from $200,000 to $4 million. L³, a firm specializing in reaching the Asian population, designed a campaign aimed at Korean and Chinese immigrants.

This case is presented to demonstrate the growth in Asian American marketing and advertising. It will give students some sense of how fast the market is growing, its relative affluence in comparison with other minority groups, and how advertising aimed at this audience must consider the important role of culture to this group.

At the conclusion of this case, students should have an understanding of the following:

1. How the Asian American market differs from other minorities
2. Why immigrants are an important target audience
3. The importance of geographical targets in ethnic campaigns

➤ Profile of the Company

Metropolitan Life Insurance Company, headquartered in New York, is the nation's second largest insurance company. It employs over 60,000 people and reported assets of $98.74 billion in 1990.[1]

The company has a long history. It was incorporated in 1866, under the name National Traveler's Insurance Company, making it one of the nation's oldest and most well-respected insurance firms. Metropolitan Life offers disability health insurance, dental insurance, automobile insurance, and pension and retirement plans.[2]

Metropolitan Life has a number of subsidiaries, including Metropolitan Tower Life, MetLife Marketing Corporation, MetLife General Insurance Agency, and MetLife Capital Corporation. In 1984, the company launched a highly successful advertising campaign featuring characters from the Peanuts comic strip, with the tagline "Get Met. It Pays."

In the early 1980s, Metropolitan Life went in search of new markets. The company made substantial inroads into the Hispanic market in 1983 and became the leading insurer of Hispanic Americans two years later. In 1986, the insurance giant tackled the untapped Asian market. Overseas the company opened an office in Tokyo in 1987 and in Taiwan in 1989.[3]

➤ What Metropolitan Life Wanted to Accomplish

Recognizing the growing economic clout of the Asian audience, Metropolitan Life Insurance Company hired a market research firm to conduct focus group studies on Asians in 1986. The company's decision to pursue the Asian market was not based on the group's size, since Asians make up only a small percentage of the overall population. But because they tend to be better educated and have strong family values and traditions, Metropolitan Life thought they might be good prospects for insurance.

The focus group research uncovered a number of interesting differences among the different Asian populations, which can be segmented along the lines of Japanese, Korean, Chinese, Vietnamese, and Filipino. For example, it was learned that Vietnamese, who tended to be immigrants, had not yet fully grasped the concept of insurance. The notion of paying for something that was intangible and that could not be used right away was strange to people from traditionally poor backgrounds. However, they could be appealed to based on their strong sense of protection for family members. A Vietnamese immigrant who struggled to get to America, and who may have had to send for family members later, would not want to see the hard work and effort wasted because of an untimely death.

The research also found that Chinese were interested in education for their children. They would be likely to purchase insurance with cash dividends that could be used later to pay for a college education.

Metropolitan Life wanted to penetrate the small but affluent Asian market. Several years prior to conducting research on this group, the insurance company conducted a similar campaign with Hispanic audiences. The success of that effort (Met Life became the primary insurance company used by Hispanics) prompted the firm to attempt the same strategies in penetrating the Asian market. The overriding goal was to sell insurance to the Asian market without offending them.

Concept/Theme Development

Metropolitan Life made the decision to pursue the Chinese and Korean markets first and to wait until later to target the Vietnamese audience. It hired L[3] to handle this sensitive account. The agency decided that before Met Life could reach the audience with its message, it needed to create awareness with the target market. Metropolitan Life was virtually unknown to the Asian community. Another insurance company, U.S. Life, was using Asian insurance salespeople to sell their products. L[3]'s first move would be to spread the word about Metropolitan Life.

The second step in the development of the advertising campaign concept was educating consumers. They needed to gain a general understanding of how insurance might benefit them and a specific knowledge about Metropolitan Life.

Finally, the ads needed to introduce and explain individual Metropolitan Life products. Once the audience understood insurance, they could be introduced to the concept of different insurance for different needs.

L[3] was careful to avoid topics considered taboo among Asians. For example, older Asians do not like to speak of or hear about death. Instead of using a straightforward approach often found in American insurance commercials (there was one in which a man was bowling one minute and in heaven the next), the agency approached the topic from a different angle. It used children instead of references to death and dying. The emphasis was placed on a positive and bright future for offspring, as opposed to a bleak and uncertain tomorrow for adults.

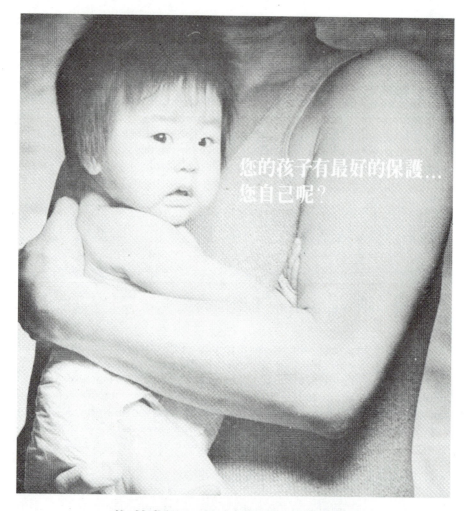

您的孩子有最好的保護...
您自己呢？

您的保障，就是您孩子的保障！

父母對子女的愛，無微不至。
任何父母都會給予自己的孩子最大的關懷和最好的
保護。不過，偉大的父母們可千萬別忘記了自己。
若您希望您的孩子安定幸福，您必需先為自己作出

保障。光特您的孩子著想是不足夠的。
大都會保險公司的營業代表經驗豐富，服務應遠傳
真，他們了解您的責任，會為您選擇一種最適合您
的保險計劃。

大都會保險公司，使您高枕無憂

壽申・保屋・健康・儲蓄人壽・退休金・互助基金

Joseph Lam, president of L^3, was aware of another problem facing an insurance company trying to sell to Asians. He pointed out that Koreans and Chinese Americans are offended by the concept of insurance. "If they are asked to buy life insurance, they will yell at you and say, 'What the hell. I'll be in my coffin already when I get the money, so I won't need the money.'"[4]

The concept development also took into account the fact that Asian people tend to be very practical. They don't like to spend their money on frivolous or meaningless items.

Metropolitan Life was using the popular Peanuts characters in its national general market campaign, an approach the insurance company and the advertising agency L^3 believed would not work for the Asian audience. Met Life's director of marketing for special projects, Reuben Lopez, said, "Chinese people aren't going to buy insurance from a dog."[5]

In summary, the concept contained several key elements. It would need to educate the consumer about insurance, focus on family protection, and avoid the subject of death.

The themes developed for the Metropolitan Life campaign grew directly from the research findings. The messages were built on the strong family values evident in the Asian community. Marriage, protection of children, and preparation for the future were the basic tenets of the Met Life campaign.

Execution

The opening campaign used the headline "Welcome to Metropolitan—Family of 43 million, an industry leader with $94 billion assets under management." Obviously, this was an effort to introduce the market to the corporation. The large numbers used in the ad (that is, 43 million and 94 billion) were designed to attract immediate attention. Because the research indicated that the target audience respected stability and dependability, the numbers let them know how many people trusted the company and how much money the firm had accumulated.

L^3 selected a variety of taglines and headlines with one basic theme: "Protect your family." One ad, in which an adult is seen holding a young baby, asks the question "You protect your child, but who protects you?" Another ad features a baby apparently taking its first steps. The copy tells parents that future security for young loved ones can be found through Metropolitan Life insurance products. Lam noted that the ad created strong emotions and pointed out the need for insurance without talking about death.

A third ad in the campaign shows a bride and groom atop a wedding cake, with the headline "Met Life and You Make the Perfect Match." It urged the newlyweds to protect their happiness and think about the future with Metropolitan Life.

The agency selected print advertisements because of the proportionately high number of Asian newspapers in the New York market. There are six Chinese newspapers operating in New York's Chinatown alone. The circulation of the three largest Chinese newspapers is estimated at 80,000. L^3 also created a full-color, glossy magazine insert for the weekend editions of the most heavily read publications.

All ads were run in Chinese. Even though there are over 300 Asian spoken dialects, the written language understood by most is Chinese.

In addition to newspapers, Metropolitan Life ads were placed in the New York subway on a route heavily traveled by Asian commuters. Based on its knowledge that 85 percent of Asian Americans own a VCR, L^3 advertised Met Life on videos made in Hong Kong but viewed in the United States.

The execution did not end with the development of advertisements. L^3 extended the campaign to include public relations and event planning. The agency created the Summer Youth Drawing Contest, an event designed to create goodwill and generate publicity for Metropolitan Life. Children between the ages of 8 and 18 are given an opportunity to draw their interpretations of the themes featured in L^3's Met Life campaign. All entries are displayed. In 1991, over 1,000 children entered the contest.

 **Conclusion**

L^3's Metropolitan Life campaign was well received. The company reported that for its initial $200,000 investment in advertising to the Asian community, it racked up $17 million in new premiums.

What is notable about L^3's approach to the campaign is that the agency took nothing for granted. It conducted research to determine the audience's receiveness to the concept of insurance. It developed a campaign based solely on the needs and desires of the target audience. The creative execution was tailor-made for the Asian audience, taking into consideration its diversity, traditions, fears, and values.

DISCUSSION QUESTIONS

1. What are the positives and negatives of not using English language in a campaign?
2. How did L^3 expand basic marketing principles to reach its target audience?

3. What are some distinct characteristics of the Asian American market?

4. How can other campaigns aimed at other ethnic immigrants use the lessons from L^3's Metropolitan Life campaign?

Endnotes

1. "Metropolitan Life Insurance Company," *International Directory of Company Histories* vol. 3 (Chicago: St. James Press, 1991), 290–294.
2. "Metropolitan Life Insurance Company," *Million Dollar Directory* (Parsippany, NJ: The Dun and Bradstreet Corporation, 1991), 3145.
3. "Metropolitan Life Insurance Company," *International Directory of Company Histories.*
4. Joseph Lam, interview by Nileeni Meegama, at L^3 Advertising Agency, New York, March 21, 1993.
5. Cathie Gandel, "Met Campaign a Showcase for Minority Marketing," *Asian Advertising and Marketing* (June, 1991): IV.

VIEW FROM THE TOP

Joseph Lam
President
L^3

In 1984, Joseph Lam and two of his associates, Wing Wan Lee and Lawrence Lee, founded the L^3 advertising agency in New York City. A native of Hong Kong, Lam has been in the United States since 1969. His advertising career includes serving as sales manager for Sino Broadcasting, the *Sino Daily Express,* and CS-TV, a Chinese television station.

Lam studied marketing and advertising at Pace University. He sits on the Board of Directors of the Chinatown Manpower Project, a nonprofit employment and training organization, and is active with the Chinese American Local Development Corporation. He has been honored for excellence and commitment by the New York City Chamber of Commerce.

L^3, listed as the only full-service Asian American advertising agency in New York, has represented Metropolitan Life, Remy Martin, Colgate–Palmolive, and Baccarat, a French crystal company.

Why did you and your partners start an Asian American advertising agency?

The mainstream market has become increasingly saturated. For a marketer to grow further he has to either go global or look into a special market. The number of Asian immigrants has been increasing annually. They are different from those who came over several decades ago, as I did. Now they come with sophistication and a vision of how to start a business and grow with it. With that in mind, we concluded that the Asian American market eventually would become one to be reckoned with. Since we have firsthand knowledge of the market because of our grassroots relationship in the community, we talked about it and decided to start our own agency in 1984.

Does your advertising agency have a particular philosophy?

L^3's philosophy for the long term is to bridge the gap between West and East. In the immediate future, we want to bridge the gap between the mainstream American marketers and the Asian American consumers. Our goal is to create a two-way street between the Asian Americans who can expand the mainstream market—since they are no longer confined to their own community—and the mainstream marketers who desperately need this affluent market and have to find ways to become part of it.

How do you segment the Asian American market? By income, education, ethnic background?

The Asian American market is a segment by itself, and, as is the Hispanic market, it is very segmented within itself. These segments include Chinese, Korean, Filipino, Japanese, Vietnamese, and Asian Indians, among others. If we break down the population into different segments we will further narrow the size of the Asian American market, thereby losing the attractiveness of the market. Many major marketers still talk only of critical mass. Research, practice, and observation have taught us that the best way to handle this situation is to look at the Asian American market as a whole, looking at its similarities rather than its differences in terms of background and demographics. Within this concept, fine-tuning cultural appeals is still possible.

Are you saying that the Asian market shouldn't be segmented?

In terms of the background and tradition, Filipinos are very different from Chinese, and Chinese, although similar to Koreans, have quite a different history. All have different temperaments and psychologies. However, we still find addressing Asian similarities more effective, logistically feasible, and less expensive than addressing their differences.

Then what approach do you take to reach this complex audience?

We know that most Asians are actually immigrants to this country. The best way to target them is to identify a common denominator, a background or interest they share. We have learned that the common denominator is the "immigrant mentality."

How do you define the "immigrant mentality"?

"Immigrant mentality" belongs to those who have come here to begin a new life. Immigrants forego much of what they had in the homeland, They are insecure; they want to be accepted; they want to blend in; they want to be recognized; and certainly, they want a better future for their children. Immigrants want stability, and America has the most stability of anyplace in the world. Immigrants are not coming here for the money anymore. Money can be made in the Far East. They come to America for a better education for the children, and they sacrifice quite a bit in terms of status and social prestige to acquire stability here. Appealing to the immigrants' emotions requires communication that is both sensitive and compelling.

What do you have to say about the stereotyping of the Asian market?

Extremes are unhelpful—viewing us as either naive or overachievers is inaccurate. Stereotypes are harmful. Advertising must strike a balance, touching on life as it is known and lived by Asians. Stereotyping, more often than not, defeats the purpose of advertising.

Do you find mainstream agencies trying to take business away from Asian agencies?

No, this market is something they don't understand. There is much that intimidates them, and the amount of money is not enough for them to interest them or make it worth their while. The budget of the Asian American market is so small compared with a mainstream project that in proportion, it's almost impossible for them to justify the cost.

Do you think that a non–Asian American has enough knowledge of the community to work effectively in an Asian advertising agency?

Here's an example. If there's a problem in a specific Chinese market and you have a Chinese individual work on it, he may not have the understanding and discipline to solve the problem. However, if you find an American who doesn't speak the language, but who has the training and discipline, and the ability to absorb first- and secondhand information, he may be able to do it. The best person to have is someone who is attached to the community culturally and linguistically and has the discipline to go through the marketing process.

Is it necessary to be Asian to work in Asian advertising?

Let's dispel the myth that a non-Asian cannot work in the Asian market. The Asian market requires knowledgeable professionals, as does any other. Although the Asian market has additional requirements for success, just being Asian is not enough. Those who understand us can market to us.

What is the future direction of your agency, and how do you think the Asian market will change in the future?

The Asian market has entered the second stage, during which more national marketers will become aware of and attracted to its potential. At the same time, competition will become increasingly fierce. Maintaining and sharpening our strategic and creative skills is our fundamental principle. However, to equip our agency to meet the challenges of the new era, we began consolidating our below-the-line capabilities. Given the inadequate availability of Asian media and the close-knit nature of the community, below-the-line disciplines such as event marketing, public relations, promotion, and merchandising will make up more than half of the battlefield in the Asian market for years to come. Most of all, we are mindful of the quality of our staff, since the Asian advertising industry is still relatively new. Continuous training to ensure that our staff possesses the requisite skills and integrity is essential for our agency to excel.

5

Uptown Cigarettes Blow Up Before They're Lit

Client: RJ Reynolds Tobacco Company
Agency: FCB/Leber Katz Partners
           New York
Target: African American cigarette smokers

This case discusses how a major cigarette manufacturer completely misjudged the market-place in developing a cigarette aimed at black consumers. The company perceived its efforts as just another target marketing strategy, but the African American community saw it as an unethical corporate behavior aimed at killing many of its members.

RJ Reynolds launched this venture without a clear understanding of the backlash it would receive from religious and social organizations opposing the sale of cigarettes and liquor to black consumers. After spending an exorbitant amount of resources developing the product, negative publicity and community pressure forced RJ Reynolds to pull the cigarette from the test market before it ever hit the shelves.

At the end of this case, students should have an understanding of the following:

1. Sensitivity of ethnic audiences to specific product lines and services
2. How research led RJ Reynolds to faulty conclusions
3. The pitfalls involved with target marketing, that is, what can go wrong
4. Problems with marketing a socially unpopular product

L---▷ Profile of the Company

The tobacco industry is an estimated $40 billion business in America. It is also extremely competitive, with one share point representing $250 million.[1]

RJ Reynolds Tobacco Company is a subsidiary of RJR Nabisco Holdings Group, Inc., the world's largest manufacturer of consumer packaged goods. An estimated 57 percent of the company's sales and 77 percent of its operating income were produced by tobacco in 1991.[2] Despite campaigns to stop smoking and a fall in the perceived popularity of smoking among the general population in the United States, worldwide tobacco sales for RJR rose 6 percent in 1991, with sales reported at a staggering $9.03 billion.[3] There was a rise of 5 percent in domestic sales in 1991.

RJR Nabisco also manufactures Planters Peanuts, Oreo cookies, and Ritz crackers. Its gross revenue climbed from $12 billion in 1989 to $15.7 billion in 1992.[4] In the late 1980s, the company lost market share to Phillip Morris, manufacturers of Virginia Slims and Marlboro, and to Lorillard, makers of Newport. In 1989, only three full-priced cigarettes gained market share, and all three were manufactured by either Morris or Lorillard. RJR's Salem brand, the nation's leading menthol cigarette, dropped an estimated 1.7 percentage points in market share between 1985 and 1989.[5]

L---▷ What RJ Reynolds Wanted to Accomplish

Although annual smoking was decreasing at a rate of around 2 percent per year, African American smoking continued to rise, making them an ideal target market for a product seeking new users. With nearly 400 brands of cigarettes on the market, African American smokers had plenty of choices. A number of cigarettes were aimed at specific audiences. Marlboros were positioned as a cigarette for people who enjoy a real smoke; Virginia Slims were for liberated women. No brand was directed only at the black smoker.

Research into the smoking patterns of African Americans indicated that almost three-quarters of black smokers select menthol brands.[6] RJ Reynolds manufactured the menthol cigarette Salem, but the product was losing ground to Lorillard's Newport. Reynolds was after the black smoker who wanted a menthol brand but found Salem too heavy.

When RJ Reynolds planned to introduce Uptown, information about black smoking behavior and the related health risks was widely available. According to 1989 government estimates, 39 percent of black males smoked, as opposed to 29 percent for the rest of the population.[7] The lung cancer rate among black males was 55 percent higher than that of white males. African American males were the group most likely to be affected by cigarette-related illnesses. In 1989, of the 50 million smokers in the country, 6 million were black.[8]

The company planned to test market Uptown in Philadelphia in September of 1989 and to release the product for national distribution later.

Concept/Theme Development

In the case of Uptown, the product's name was an integral part of the overall marketing strategy. "Uptown" is a word with significant social and cultural relevance for urban African Americans. It is used to describe upward mobility; it is a place to which black people aspire. The famous Apollo Theatre is uptown. The Harlem Renaissance took place uptown. There was a popular black movie in the 1970s called *Uptown Saturday Night*. In black colloquialism, uptown is a place where the action is and where the party people go.

FCB/Leber Katz Partners was given the Uptown account. The agency's primary objective was to create a campaign that appealed to African American smokers' lifestyles. Because such a large proportion of the African American community smoked, the campaign would need to have broad-based appeal. For lower-income black smokers, the product would represent a step up toward a more sophisticated lifestyle. For middle-income smokers, Uptown was indicative of the type of life they perceived themselves to be leading. Upscale smokers could easily identify with the product—with a name like Uptown, it must be aimed at them.

The agency settled on the theme "Uptown, the place. The taste." Body copy read, "A lighter menthol flavor than our major menthol brand Salem . . . allowing more menthol taste to come through." The Uptown ad thus answered all the pertinent questions consumers were likely to ask about a new product. The black smokers' preference for menthol was addressed. The product was immediately distinguished from Salem, and it was not directly compared to any competitive brand, therefore indicating that it was in a league of its own.

➤ Execution

Because Uptown cigarettes were never introduced to the general market, the advertising campaign was not executed. The only ad made available showed a young and attractive black couple, happily strolling down a big city street at night. They were stylishly dressed and looking back toward the camera. They were obviously having a good time and enjoying the taste of Uptown cigarettes.

➤ Conclusion

Before the scheduled Philadelphia market test, Uptown and RJ Reynolds found themselves surrounded by controversy. The company and the product faced intense pressure from African American leaders. Most notably, Secretary of Health and Human Services Louis Sullivan openly criticized RJ Reynolds. He called the campaign "slick and sinister advertising . . . cynically and deliberately targeted toward black Americans."[9] Other community leaders followed Sullivan's lead, and within days, RJ Reynolds announced that it would withdraw the brand. The cost of canceling the test is estimated at between $5 and $7 million.

RJ Reynolds was accused of being stupid for honestly announcing its intention to specifically target blacks. Others said RJ Reynolds was too quick to back down, making it more difficult for other cigarette manufacturers to go after special audiences.

Not all African Americans agreed that the brand should have been withdrawn. Veteran advertising executive Caroline Jones told *Advertising Age* that it would be worse for advertisers to ignore black consumers than to target them, no matter what product they are marketing.[10] Black newspapers, heavily dependent on cigarette advertising, also saw the withdrawal of Uptown as a financial blow. Further confounding the situation was the fact that RJ Reynolds had poured a considerable amount of money into the black community through promotions, contests, and concert sponsorship.

An *Advertising Age* editorial asked the provocative question "Should RJ Reynolds or other tobacco marketers be effectively barred by the government from designing and promoting cigarette brands meant to appeal to blacks? Or to women? No, not as long as cigarettes are legal."[11]

Despite the failure of Uptown cigarettes, RJ Reynolds continued to produce and plan brands aimed at specific target audiences. The Dakota brand was to be aimed at young, less-educated, blue-collar white women. Like Uptown, Dakota cigarettes never reached the marketplace.

In 1990, RJ Reynolds produced a cigarette called Salem Gold. The company said that the new product was unlike Uptown because it contained different tar and nicotine levels. Like Uptown, Salem Gold was a mentholated brand, lighter in taste than the traditional Salem. Billboard advertising for Salem Gold used the line "Max taste. Less chill." The ads ran in both Spanish and English. Minority community advocates again criticized RJ Reynolds, claiming the company simply reintroduced Uptown in a different package. The cigarette manufacturer denied the claims.

DISCUSSION QUESTIONS ◄-------------------------------

1. Could RJ Reynolds have introduced this brand in any manner that would have gained acceptance by the black audience?
2. Did the company make the right decision in pulling the brand?
3. Could research have indicated the backlash to the product?
4. Is RJ Reynolds an unethical company, or does it have the right to market its products to all consumers?
5. What, if anything, is different about targeting a product to an ethnic group than to the general population?

Endnotes

1. Judann Dagnoli, "RJR's Uptown Targets Blacks," *Advertising Age* (18 December 1989): 4.
2. "RJR Nabisco Holdings Corporation," *Moody's Handbook of Common Stocks* (New York: Moody's Investors Service, Spring 1993).
3. Ibid.
4. Ibid.
5. Dagnoli, "RJR's Uptown Targets Blacks," 44.
6. Centers for Disease Control, "Cigarette Brand Use Among Adult Smokers—United States, 1986," *Morbidity and Mortality Weekly Report* 39, no. 665 (1990): 671–673.
7. Boyd G. Schoenborn, "Smoking and Other Tobacco Use: United States, 1987" (Washington, D.C.: U.S. Department of Health and Human Services, Public Health Service, National Centers for Health Statistics, 1987).
8. Alcohol, Drug Abuse, and Mental Health Administration, "National Institute on Drug Abuse, National Household Survey on Drug Abuse: Population Estimates 1988" (Washington, D.C.: U.S. Department of Health Service, Alcohol, Drug Abuse, and Mental Health Administration, 1989).
9. "Uptown Goes Down," *Science* 247 (2 February 1990): 530
10. Dagnoli, "RJR's Uptown Targets Blacks," 4.
11. "The Downing of Uptown," *Advertising Age* (29 January 1990): 32.

VIEW FROM THE TOP

Adriane T. Gaines

Executive Director
World Institute of Black Communications

The World Institute of Black Communications, Inc., is a nonprofit organization established to formally recognize and encourage excellence in communicating information to and about African Americans. The Communications Excellence to Black Audiences (CEBA) awards were established in 1979 by the institute. The awards honor advertising agencies, corporations, and individuals who have demonstrated sensitivity and understanding in addressing the African American consumer market.

Adriane T. Gaines, the executive director and co-founder of the CEBA awards, coordinates the annual judging. She is a graduate of Fordham University with a bachelor's degree in communications and has attended the New York Institute of Technology. She is a member of the Board of Trustees, Apollo Theatre Hall of Fame; a board member of the Central Harlem Senior Citizens Center; a board member of the Coalition of 100 Black Women; a member of the New York Women's Foundation; a member of the Corporate Advisory Council of the Schomburg Center for Research in Black Culture; and a board member of Aaron Davis Hall. In 1985, she received the Media Woman of the Year honor from the National Association of Media Women.

Why were the CEBA awards founded?

In 1978, the year we created the awards, the images of blacks in advertising were appalling. We wanted to create a vehicle by which advertising could be monitored, judged, and rewarded. We established the awards to pay tribute to agencies and individuals who, through their work, demonstrate integrity and excellence.

How does the competition work?

We get literally thousands of entries each year. Last year we received 5,000 entries. They come from advertising agencies, marketing departments, and others associated with the communications process. Eligibility is based on whether the work was published, aired, or displayed during the previous calendar year. Decisions are made by a panel of distinguished judges from the industry. Believe me, it's a tough job.

What are the award categories?

Categories include consumer print, radio, television commercials, video and cable programming, merchandising and sales promotion, and corporate or institutional awards. There are 47 categories in all. Awards are given for excellence, distinction, or merit.

What are the judges looking for?

The entries are judged on a number of criteria. Creative execution and positive imagery are high on the list. The judges also look at positioning; that is, does the selling message effectively target the product or service to the African American consumer? In image, we are looking for a positive reflection of African American values and attitudes. We also want the ad to be relevant: It should reflect an understanding of African American experiences. Finally, we want to know if the ad works; that is, does it make the viewer or reader want to purchase the product.

Have there been any changes to the awards in recent years?

In 1991, we added the CEBA Corporate Award to honor companies with outreach programs that have helped in the economic or social well-being of the black community. The effort is judged on planning and research, execution, presentation, and results. It's a very prestigious award. The first Corporate Award of excellence went to the Nestlé Corporation, for its *Men of Courage* book, an 84-page publication featuring moving stories about 34 black American men who beat the odds. That year, we also honored 13 black filmmakers for their contributions to African American society. We want to encourage the continuance of black films.

How have the images you see each year changed since 1978?

They are 100 percent improved over what we first saw. We see black people in family settings, on picnics, at family reunions. Black people travel, consume name brand products, and use credit cards. In the 1970s, the images were much more stereotypical.

The distinctive CEBA statuette has been donated to the Smithsonian Institution's Anacostia Museum. What does the statue represent?

Sculptress Valerie Maynard designed the statue. The two faces reflect the duality of the African American experience. The long aristocratic neck demonstrates the spirit of Mother Africa. The arms are placed in a protective embrace. The spear represents power; a globe is at the crown, and the CEBA signature graces the base. The statue is made of molten steel and burnished in bronze. It is a beautiful representation of the award.

Is it possible for a cigarette or liquor manufacturer to create a positive advertising campaign aimed at African Americans?

We have a category for these products. It's no secret that black consumers use both cigarettes and liquor. The job of the World Institute is not to judge the products, but to deal strictly with the execution of the message. Many of the ads entered from these types of companies are dealing with corporate and institutional messages. It is hoped they will be viewed objectively in this context.

The stanza form is almost certainly Traherne's own choice, for he followed Herbert in the invention of new ones for nearly every poem, but once having determined upon it he seems to feel its confining character. Instead of the freedom to chant "the Streets were mine, The Temple was mine, the people were mine" he is apparently faced with the necessity to write a line of tetrameter, a line of trimeter, and then one of pentameter within which he must find a rhyme for "mine" because, in conventional verse, two or three "mines" in a row are not allowed. Thus, the ten syllables of the third line seem pushed into place behind the inevitable "shine," and the spontaneous directness in the *Centuries* of "Sparkling Eys fair Skins and ruddy faces"—which here becomes "Oh how did all their Lovly faces shine!"—is lost behind the wall of foot length and rhyme scheme.

A similar falling off of poetic character takes place in the last four lines of the stanza where Traherne inserts a brief catalogue—"Joy, Beauty, Welfare"—that has no apparent principle of order, traps himself into several lines of awkward syntax, and ends with a rather neutral four-syllable line, "Adornd the Ground," that has what seems to be an unintentionally ambiguous connection with the preceding syntax. The difficulty does not appear to spring from any basic inability to write a proper line of verse but rather from Traherne's desire to write in a repetitive, biblical form. He tends almost always to ignore the demands of conventional verse structure and to avoid the integrated metaphoric image, for the images he seeks are those that demonstrate the oneness of all in God. He is indifferent to the rhetorical devices through which the working out of temporal relations is conventionally achieved. The vision he refers to in this stanza is "like an Angel," and it sees the streets as though they were paved with gold, but this is a commonplace description rather than a metaphor, and the statements in the stanza are related not metaphorically, but adjectivally and statically by holding a mirror up to things and reflecting their eternal gloriousness without relating one to another. When Traherne tries to confine his repetitive structures to conventional verse, its inappropriateness for them and for the vision they are designed to express often appears as awkward, flat, and "unpoetic" lines. In "The Improvement," for example, the perception of everything in one vast, divine unity focused in the soul is expressed characteristically:

5

His Wisdom, Goodness, Power, as they unite
All things in one, that they may be the *Treasures*
Of one *Enjoy'r,* shine in the utmost Height
They can attain; and are most Glorious *Pleasures,*
    When all the Univers conjoynd in one,
    Exalts a Creature, as if that alone.

6

To bring the Moisture of far distant Seas
Into a *point,* to make them present here,
In *virtu,* not in *Bulk*; one man to pleas
With all the *Powers* of the Highest Sphere,
    From East, from West, from North and South, to bring
    The pleasing *Influence* of evry thing;

7

Is far more *Great* then to Creat them there
Where now they stand; His *Wisdom* more doth shine
In that, his *Might* and *Goodness* more appear,
In recollecting; He is more *Divine*
    In making evry Thing a Gift to one
    Then in the Parts of all his Spacious *Throne.*

                   ("The Improvement," 25–42)

Here there is no metaphoric contract, no organized connotative unity toward which the rhyme scheme, rhythmic pattern, and other devices are pointing. Instead there is the force of the thought that expresses itself in complex but balanced and repeated structures, and the conventional stanza lines seem to be rather like the "Churlish Proprieties . . . Bounds. . .[and] Divisions" which represent for him the "Dirty Devices of this World" (*CM* III.3) that he must unlearn. The thought, the idea of the poem, becomes the paramount concern, and whatever connotative process its expression may entail becomes absorbed by the repetitive, parallel units of thought as we see when the lines are rearranged:

To bring the Moisture of far distant Seas Into a *point*,
  to make them present here, in *virtu,* not in *Bulk*;
One man to pleas with all the *Powers* of the Highest Sphere,
        from East,
        from West,
        from North and South,
    To bring the pleasing *Influence* of evry thing;
      Is far more Great
      Then to Creat them there Where now they stand;
  His *Wisdom* more doth shine In that
  his *Might* and *Goodness* more appear In recollecting;
  He is more *Divine*
    In making evry Thing a Gift to one
  Then in the Ports of all his Spacious *Throne*.

To see Traherne's lines arranged in this way makes their paralleling, repetitive form immediately apparent and demonstrates their lack of metaphor, and it suggests not only the answer to why he was a more successfully "poetic" writer of prose than of conventional verse but also the probability that had he been able to shape the conventional verse line into the form he needed to express his unitive vision he might have become one of poetry's great originals, as did Whitman. Gay Wilson Allen has made observations about Whitman and the backgrounds of his poetry that have remarkable appropriateness for Traherne as well:

But though this psychology ["of the expanding ego"] may be called the background or basic method of Whitman's poetic technique, the catalog itself . . . emerged only after he had found a verse structure appropriate for expressing his cosmic inspiration and democratic sentiment. Nowhere in the universe does he recognize caste or subordination. Everything is equally perfect and equally divine. He admits no supremes, or rather insists that "There can be any number of supremes."

The expression of such doctrines demands a form in which units are co-ordinate, distinctions eliminated, all flowing together in a synonymous or "democratic" structure. He needed a grammatical and rhetorical structure which would be cumulative in effect rather than logical or progressive.

Possibly, as many critics have believed, he found such a structure in the primitive rhythms of the King James Bible. . . . The structure of Hebraic poetry, even in English translation, is almost lacking in subordination.[9]

When Traherne wrote in prose, his natural sensitivity to rhythm, sound, and image guided him securely, and his work takes on all the qualities that Allen here attributes to Whitman. When Traherne wrote in poetry, the models of traditional versification that were available to him were, however, too strong to overturn, and that is why his poetry contains many isolated phrases and whole stanzas of considerable beauty and tightness of construction, but not as many fully integrated whole poems. It is also why Traherne's poetic practice is primarily symbolic and abstract rather than metaphoric and concrete and why he often seems to be arbitrary in his choice of words and unplanned or "open" in terms of structure. His poetry cannot be explained or justified simply by uncovering his mystical thought (for that thought is also fully expressed in his prose) nor by calling attention to his tendency to destroy, through abstractions and repetitions, the integrity of "limits and boundaries." Traherne was a mystic and both in prose and in poetry he did seek to demonstrate the falseness of the limiting illusion; but what must finally be explained is why there is so noticeable a difference between the level of mastery in such prose as meditation three of Century Three and the level of the best of the poetry, whichever poem we may wish to call his best. The explanation lies in the freedom Traherne felt to pursue in prose the repetitive forms that were natural to the expression of his vision. In poetry he was restricted by the conventional forms of verse that were the inheritance of his historical age.

Traherne's Felicities

But all of this is not to deny that much of Traherne's poetry is admirable and effective, especially for the reader who can participate with Traherne in the excitement of contemplating highly abstract, metaphysical ideas. It is about the meaning of these for the soul in its quest for the ultimate perception of God that Traherne always writes—even when he seems to be interested in the concrete or the sensual experience. In "The Odour," for example, which exists in Philip's version alone, there is strong sensual imagery relating to the body, based upon the Song of Songs, but it is, characteristically, the spiritual meaning of any sense perception, its *use,* that is finally Traherne's real concern:

> Like Amber fair thy Fingers grow;
> With fragrant Hony-sucks thy Head is crown'd;
> Like Stars, thine Eys; thy Cheeks like Roses shew:
>   All are Delights profound.
> Talk with thy self; thy self enjoy and see:
> At once the Mirror and the Object be.
>
> What's Cinnamon, compar'd to thee?
> Thy Body is than Cedars better far:
> Those Fruits and Flowers which in Fields I see,
>   With *Thine,* can not compare.
> Where ere thou movest, there the Scent I find
> Of fragrant Myrrh and Aloes left behind.
>
> But what is Myrrh? What Cinnamon?
> What Aloes, Cassia, Spices, Hony, Wine?
> O sacred *Uses*! You to think upon
>   Than these I more incline.
> To see, taste, smell, observ; is to no End,
> If I *the Use* of each don't apprehend.
>
> ("The Odour," 49–66)

The poem as a whole is not quite equal to these stanzas, which do not seem marred by the conflict between Traherne's repetitive form and traditional verse conventions; but even here we are not allowed to dwell long on the sense detail and are asked instead to seek its spiritual meaning and to contemplate its intelligible idea.

Stanley Stewart has made analyses of several poems that exist only in the Burney manuscript and called attention to the interesting thought and beauties of such poems as "Shadows in the Water" and "On Leaping over the Moon."[10] These poems are admirable even though we cannot know precisely how much altered they are by Philip's editing, and they are an integral part of the progress of ideas as the Burney sequence unfolds from the vision of innocence through the soul's apostasy and its gradual recognition in maturity of what that vision is and means. But as an example of what poetic heights Traherne could rise to, it is well to choose a poem from the Dobell group wherein we know the lines can be trusted. An excellent illustrative poem is "The Rapture." It is brief and successful and in Traherne's best ecstatic style. It also invites comparison with the lyrics of William Blake. Traherne writes:

1

Sweet Infancy!
O fire of Heaven! O Sacred Light!
How Fair and Bright!
How Great am I,
Whom all the World doth magnifie!

2

O Heavenly Joy!
O Great and Sacred Blessedness,
Which I possess!
So great a Joy
Who did into my Armes convey!

3

From GOD abov
Being sent, the Heavens me enflame,
To prais his Name.
The Stars do move!
The Burning Sun doth shew his Love.

4

O how Divine
Am I! To all this Sacred Wealth,
This Life and Health,
Who raisd? Who mine
Did make the same? What Hand Divine!

("The Rapture," 1–20)

The short phrases that run throughout the poem celebrate the infant vision and imitate the wonder felt at the splendor of the newly discovered world. Instead of seeking at once to explain or to grasp the Creation with the categorizing function of the mind, the infant soul simply "apprehends" or contemplates it in an act of pure admiration that asks only what the source of it is: "So great a Joy / Who did into my Armes convey!" The brightness, the wealth, and the splendor of the Creation so fill the soul's attention that it is inflamed with the "fire of Heaven" and magnified by its "Sacred Light" which is reflected in the natural things of the world. The language here enhances a sense of the almost overwhelming richness of the vision, as if the soul is "burning" with its "blessedness," as the sun is burning in its demonstration of God's love. The connotations of these images work in harmony even though that harmony is based upon a broad and general sense of bright, sacred beauty. We see no objects clearly in their detail, but through the short phrases that mention those objects we are given a cumulative effect of similar associations or impressions without a connective logic between them. We have something like a series of snapshots of temporally disconnected but thematically similar things. Like the natural world to which the infant soul is responding, all of the separate things add up to one glorious meaning, but their source always remains the fundamental mystery of our existence: "To all this Sacred Wealth, / This Life and Health, / Who raisd? Who mine / Did make the same? What Hand Divine?"

Thus, as in Traherne's work generally, a surface simplicity, the perspective of a child's open wonder at the Creation, masks a profound insight into the mystery of Being and Existence, eternity and time, the many and the One. The individual soul (the many) is shown by the gloriousness of the universe, which it possesses and to which it also belongs, that it is "part of" the One that is its ultimate source:

> Sweet Infancy!
> O fire of Heaven! O Sacred Light!
>   How Fair and Bright!
>   How Great am I,
> Whom all the World doth magnifie!

And this combination of simplicity with deep mystery is achieved here through the ecstatic expostulations of a child who is filled with the splendor of the Creation and feels its secret meaning but does not connect things with each other in terms of temporal logic. In this brief lyric Traherne has expressed everything that is essential to his whole unitive vision, and the repetitive, paralleling structures (here appearing as short expostulations) work perfectly with the conventional rhyme scheme and line length partly because there is little connectedness between those objects that the infant sees. The poem is reminiscent of

Blake's "The Lamb" in its childlike questioning of the nature of experience, but if we look at only a stanza or two of Blake's poem, its stronger temporal logic, its clearer statement of the relationship of things in a sequential process, is immediately apparent:

Little Lamb who made thee?
Dost thou know who made thee?
Gave thee life & bid thee feed,
By the stream & o'er the mead;
Gave thee clothing of delight,
Softest clothing wooly bright;
Gave thee such a tender voice,
Making all the vales rejoice:
Little Lamb, who made thee
Dost thou know who made thee?[11]

We may perhaps prefer Blake's more fully connotative statement, but Traherne's innocent lyric, by virtue of the techniques we have seen throughout his work, moves us more directly and immediately into the mystery of Being itself. Traherne possesses in highest degree that ability to give us a direct experience of the infinite, eternal reality in which we exist, and when those repetitive devices that are natural to his prose are in harmony with the structures of lyric poetry—as they are in "The Rapture"—that experience is unequalled for ecstatic beauty and excitement. For many readers it may be that those moments of harmony are relatively rare, but it is at least clear that they are achieved by a blending of the regular verse line with an incantatory naming of the inexhaustible riches of the universe, placed (like exquisite jewels in their setting) forever in the infinite, eternal Mind of God. All of the devices of repetition that we have discovered Traherne working with in his most characteristic prose are, thus, also the most potent forces shaping his poetry, but, curiously, they are as much responsible for his failures, when they are in conflict with inherited poetic conventions, as they are responsible for his successes, when they are in harmony with the structures of lyric verse as he knew them. We have seen many other characteristics in Traherne's work, but this one quality, the direct sensation of eternity, can be traced like an unbroken thread through almost everything he wrote.

Notes and References

Chapter One

1. See H. M. Margoliouth, ed., *Thomas Traherne: Centuries, Poems, and Thanksgivings,* 2 vols. (Oxford, 1958), 1:xxiii–xxxvii. Additional items of chronology and attribution can be found in several papers by Carol Marks, especially "Traherne's Church's Year-Book," *Papers of the Bibliographical Society of America* 60 (1966): 31–72; Anne Ridler, "Traherne: Some Wrong Attributions," *Review of English Studies* 18 (February 1967): 48–49; and [Richard] Lynn Sauls, "Traherne's Hand in the Credenhill Records," *The Library* 24 (1969): 50. For the reader's convenience, all references to biographical data which Margoliouth includes will be referred to his edition. Gladys Wade, *Thomas Traherne: A Critical Biography* (Princeton, 1944), is sometimes helpful although her speculative and sentimental approach to biographical "facts" is a serious flaw.

2. Margoliouth, 1: xxxvii.

3. *Athenae Oxonienses* (1691–92), in Margoliouth, 1: xxiii; and *Miscellanies* (1696), in Margoliouth, 1: xxviii.

4. From the Lambeth Palace Library MS. 998, in Margoliouth, 1: xxiv.

5. Margoliouth, 1: xxxvi.

6. As Sauls points out in his note on Traherne's signature in the Credenhill records, the parish register (which is complete from 1662 through the years Traherne could have been there) is signed by him for the first time in 1664. He signed it thereafter in 1665, 1667, and 1668. The Brasenose College Register also contains an interesting though equivocal note. Immediately after the record of his receiving the M.A. in November 1661 is written, "readm. 9 Dec." (Margoliouth, 1: xxiv). In view of this note and the fact that Traherne's hand does not appear in the Credenhill records until 1664, it is surprising that Margoliouth could say that Traherne "resided at Credenhill as rector from 1661–1669" (1: xxxvii). What evidence there is suggests, instead, a residency from 1664–1668/9.

7. Wade makes this speculation, which may have some merit, but she romanticizes Traherne's social position in order to present him as "an obscure Herefordshire rector" who was offered a "highly coveted. . . post" by the "eminent lawyer" and Lord Keeper, Sir Orlando Bridgeman. See Wade, p. 87.

8. See Wade, pp. 87, 112. Marks, in her edition (with George Guffey) of *Christian Ethicks* (Ithaca, 1968), says that Finch's wife "belonged to the Harvey family of Herefordshire, of which . . . Mrs. Hopton was a member" (p. xxviii, n. 43), but the articles in the *Dictionary of National Biography* for Susanna Hopton and Heneage Finch (the younger) claim that Mrs. Hopton's family was from Staffordshire and that Finch married an Elizabeth Harvey, sister of Daniel Harvey, a London merchant.

9. Dobell, in the introduction to his edition of the poems (reprinted in Wade's 1932 edition), helped draw a picture of Traherne as a simple and naturally happy child of God, a picture that has been difficult to alter: "The poet was, it is plain, one of those rare and enviable individuals in whom no jarring element is present, who come into the world as into their rightful inheritance, and whose life is a song of thankfulness for the happiness which they enjoy in it." In Gladys Wade, ed., *The Poetical Works of Thomas Traherne* (London, 1932; reprinted, New York, 1965), p. lvi. Wade, of course, echoes this in her biography, p. 3.

10. From the preface to the *Thanksgivings,* printed anonymously by Reverend Doctor Hicks as *A Serious and Pathetical Contemplation of the Mercies of God, in Several Most Devout and Sublime Thanksgivings for the Same* (London: Samuel Keble, 1699). In Margoliouth, 1: xxxii.

11. Margoliouth, 1: xxviii.

12. All references to *Centuries of Meditations,* unless otherwise noted, are from the Margoliouth edition and will be cited in the text by century and meditation number, as above.

13. Douglas Bush, *English Literature in the Earlier Seventeenth Century,* 2d ed. (New York: Oxford University Press, 1962), p. 158.

14. Marks, "Year-Book," pp. 71–72.

15. Quoted from *Major Poets of the Earlier Seventeenth Century,* Barbara Lewalski and Andrew Sabol, eds. (New York: The Odyssey Press, 1973).

16. For a valuable analysis of how the new Restoration Anglican writers and preachers were shaping the attitude toward reason, see Irene Simon, *Three Restoraton Divines: Barrow, South, Tillotson* (Paris: Société d'Edition Les Belles Lettres, 1967), esp. "Chapter Two: Anglican Rationalism in the Seventeenth Century."

17. Joseph Glanvill, *The Vanity of Dogmatizing: The Three 'Versions',* ed. Stephen Medcalf (Hove, Sussex: The Harvester Press, 1970) pp. 226–27.

18. Ibid., sig. A3r.

19. *The Works of that Eminent and Most Learned Prelate, Dr. Edward Stillingfleet,* 6 vols. (London: J. Hepstinstall, 1707–10), 5: A4v.

20. G. R. Cragg, *From Puritanism to the Age of Reason: A Study of Changes in Religious Thought Within the Church of England 1660 to 1700* (Cambridge: At the University Press, 1950), p. 34.

21. Helen C. White, Ruth C. Wallerstein, and Ricardo Quintana, eds., *Seventeenth-Century Verse and Prose,* 2 vols. (New York: Macmillan Company, 1952), 2:9.

22. Quoted by Cragg, p. 34.

23. South advises, for example, "That the *Voice* of Reason, in all the Dictates of *Natural Morality,* ought carefully to be attended to," and Tillotson asserts "that virtue and vice are not arbitrary things . . . there is a natural and immutable and eternal reason for that which we call goodness and virtue." In White et al., 2:196, 202.

24. C. S. Lewis, *The Discarded Image: An Introduction to Medieval and Renaissance Literature* (Cambridge: At the University Press, 1970), p. 157. Lewis is here quoting from Thomas Aquinas, in part.

25. See Robert Hoopes, *Right Reason in the English Renaissance* (Cambridge: Harvard University Press, 1962), pp. 21–22.

26. Cragg, pp. 63–64.

27. Ernst Cassirer, *The Platonic Renaissance in England,* trans. James P. Pettegrove (Austin: University of Texas Press, 1953), pp. 60–61.

28. Nathanael Culverwell, *An Elegant and Learned Discourse of the Light of Nature, with Severall Other Treatises* (London: John Rothwel, 1654), p. 5.

29. Benjamin Whichcote, *Moral and Religious Aphorisms,* Number 644, in *The Cambridge Platonists,* C. A. Patrides, ed. (Cambridge: Harvard University Press, 1970), p. 332. Hereafter cited as Patrides, *Platonists*.

30. Glanvill, p. 104.

31. Ibid., p. 105.

32. Henry More, *Enthusiasmus Triumphatus,* sec. 63, quoted by Aharon Lichtenstein, *Henry More: The Rational Theology of a Cambridge Platonist* (Cambridge: Harvard University Press, 1962), pp. 77–78.

33. Marks, "Thomas Traherne's Early Studies," p. 518.

34. See William T. Costello, *The Scholastic Curriculum at Early Seventeenth-Century Cambridge* (Cambridge: Harvard University Press, 1958) for an enlightening discussion of the part such scholastic practices played in the life of students at Cambridge (as well as Oxford) shortly before and into Traherne's time.

35. Barbara J. Shapiro, *John Wilkins, 1614–1672: An intellectual Biography* (Berkely: University of California Press, 1969), p. 123. The book is an excellent description of the lively state of scientific study at Wadham as

well as the whole of Oxford. See also Mark H. Curtis, *Oxford and Cambridge in Transition: 1558–1642* (Oxford: Clarendon Press, 1959), pp. 227–60.

36. Shapiro, p. 133.

37. Ibid., p. 129.

38. As Stanley Fish phrases it in a discussion of this issue in *Self-Consuming Artifacts: The Experience of Seventeenth-Century Literature* (Berkeley: University of California Press, 1972), p. 381.

39. Edward Fowler (1632–1714), an apologist for the Latitudinarians, provides an excellent example of how contemporary intellectuals understood what it was these men were thinking. In *The Principles and Practices of Certain Moderate Divines of the Church of England, (greatly mis-understood) Truly Represented and Defended* (London: Lodowick Lloyd, 1670), Fowler takes a position that is clearly an application of deductive reason to religion. Although his tone is much drier and more deistic than Traherne's, Fowler expresses Traherne's position that by the use of reason man can "*draw clear Inferences from evident Principles,*" that these "self-evident Principles of the Gospel" (p. 70) tell us that "the imitation of the Divine Nature, is the whole design of the Christian Religion" (p. 72), and that even though its genuine mysteries make it more than a merely "natural" religion, Christianity's reasonableness "makes it a Religion as easie to be practised by Mankinde as can be: for all the Duties, wherein consisteth the substance of it must have continued to oblige us, whether they were therein expressed or no" (p. 92).

40. All references to *Christian Ethicks* are from the edition by Marks and Guffey and will be cited in the text as *CE* followed by page number.

41. Patrides, *Platonists,* p. 17.

42. *Hermes Mercurius Trismegistus, His Divine Pymander . . . Together with his Second Book, Called Asclepius,* trans. John Everard (London: Thomas Brewster, 1657), p. 159.

43. John Everard, *Some Gospel Treasures Opened* (London: Rapha Harford, 1653), p. 14.

44. Ibid., p. 60.

45. Thomas Vaughan, *A Hermeticall Banquet, Drest by a Spagiricall Cook* (London: Andrew Crooke, 1652), sig. B1.

46. Thomas Taylor, *Meditations from the Creatures,* 3d ed. (London: John Bartlet, 1632), p. 23.

47. Francis King, "Thomas Traherne: Intellect and Felicity," *Restoration Literature: Critical Approaches,* (London, 1972), p. 141.

48. Ibid., pp. 140–41.

49. Louis Martz, *The Paradise Within* (New Haven, 1964), p. 48. His full statement is: "Thus by cogitating, assembling, various transistory

examples of the good, the mind in meditation draws toward an inward understanding of the good."

50. See, especially, A. L. Clements, *The Mystical Poetry of Thomas Traherne* (Cambridge, 1969) and Allison J. Sherrington, *Mystical Symbolism in the Poetry of Thomas Traherne* (St. Lucia, Australia, 1970).

51. See Stanley Stewart, *The Expanded Voice: The Art of Thomas Traherne* (San Marino, CA., 1970).

52. Patrides, *Platonists,* p. 36, n. 1, provides useful information concerning the origin of this well-known statement that God is a circle whose center is everywhere and whose circumference nowhere. He writes: "This famous affirmation has been traced (by E. Gilson . . .) to an anonymous work of the twelfth century, generally known as *Liber XXIV philosophorum* and attributed to 'Hermes' by Alan of Lille and others."

Chapter Two

1. Nicholas of Cusa, *The Vision of God* (1453), trans. Emma Gurney Salter (New York: E. P. Dutton, 1928), p. 12.

2. Stewart, *Expanded Voice,* pp. 70–71.

3. See Jackson I. Cope, "Seventeenth-Century Quaker Style," in *Seventeenth Century Prose: Modern Essays in Criticism,* ed. Stanley Fish (New York: Oxford University Press, 1971), p. 200.

4. Ibid., p. 204.

5. These three "motives" for Traherne's repetitive style have been suggested respectively by Stanley Stewart, Joan Webber in *The Eloquent "I"* (Madison, WI., 1968), and Arthur Clements.

6. Pico della Mirandola, "A Platonick Discourse Written . . . In explication of a Sonnet by Hieronimo Benivieni," in Thomas Stanley, *The History of Philosophy,* 2d ed. (London: T. Bassett, 1687), p. 198. Compare Paul Kristeller, *The Philosophy of Marsilio Ficino,* trans. Virginia Conant (New York: Columbia University Press, 1943; reprint ed., Gloucester, Mass: Peter Smith, 1964), p. 246, and Eugene Rice, *The Renaissance Idea of Wisdom* (Cambridge: Harvard University Press, 1958), p. 63.

7. John Norris, *The Theory of the Ideal or Intelligble World,* 2 vols. (London: S. Manship, 1701–04; facsimile ed., Hildesheim: Georg Olms Verlag, 1974), 1:9.

8. See the excellent introduction to the *Ethicks* by Marks, especially pp. xv–xxxvi. Because of the thoroughness of this introduction it has been possible to concentrate here upon analysis of Traherne's thought and style,

but for a description of the *Ethicks* in relation to its historical and contemporary backgrounds Marks is essential.

9. Glanvill, *Dogmatizing,* pp. 143–44.

10. Aquinas also places Repentance in the Theological Virtues.

11. See the *Summa Theologica,* II, I, Q. 57, Art. 4 and Q. 61, Art. 1.

12. Book 1, 1094b, 10, W. D. Ross, trans., Great Books of the Western World, vol. 9 (Chicago: Encyclopaedia Britannica, 1952), p. 339.

13. Vivian De Sola Pinto, *Peter Sterry: Platonist and Puritan: A Biographical and Critical Study with Passages Selected from his Writings* (Cambridge: At the University Press, 1934; reprint ed., New York: Greenwood Press, 1968), p. 90.

14. *Meister Eckhart: A Modern Translation,* ed. and trans. Raymond Blakney (New York: Harper Torchbooks, 1941), p. 209.

15. Cusa, pp. 48–49.

16. Both Edgar Wind, *Pagan Mysteries in the Renaissance,* new and enl. ed. (New York: Barnes and Noble, 1968), pp. 225, 239, and John Nelson, *Renaissance Theory of Love: The Context of Giordano Bruno's 'Eroici furori'* (New York: Columbia University Press, 1958), p. 256, n. 19, make this point.

17. Cusa, pp. 19, 117.

18. *The Philosophy of Love* (1535), trans. F. Friedeberg-Seeley and Jean H. Barnes with an introduction by Cecil Roth (London: Soncino Press, 1937), pp. 45–46.

19. Consider, also, the words of Meister Eckhart as quoted by Ananda K. Coomaraswamy, *Time and Eternity* (Ascona, Switzerland: Artibus Asiae, 1947), p. 124:

"to have all that has being and is lustily to be desired and brings delight; to have it simultaneously and partless. . . in the soul entire and that in God, revealed in its unveiled perfection, where first it burgeons forth and in the ground of its essence, and all there grasped where God grasps himself,—that is happiness."

20. Plotinus, *Ennead,* 2.9.16, says, for example: "To despise this Sphere, and the Gods within it or anything else that is lovely, is not the way to goodness." (*Plotinus: The Six Enneads,* trans., Stephen MacKenna and B. S. Page, Great Books of the Western World, vol. 17 (Chicago: Encyclopaedia Britannica, 1952), p. 76.

21. It must always be kept in mind that, in a sense, when Traherne speaks of many souls he is speaking in the language of "accommodation," or symbolically, for "there is no other approach to a knowledge of things divine than that of symbols." [Nicholas Cusanus, *Of Learned Ignorance,* trans. Germain Heron (New Haven: Yale University Press, 1954), p. 27.]

It is only the symbolic, "provisional" use of language, where statements are true in one way and untrue in another, that can express the proper understanding of the integral nature of both the essential (in essence) and the existential (in existence) planes. Traherne's basically metaphysical and esoteric mode of thinking assumes an identity of God and the soul on the essential plane (in fact *must* do so if God is pure Being—the Intelligible World), but of course also recognizes otherness on the plane of existence (the world of manifestation). As Cusa says, in another expression of the Intelligible World concept: "In it [the Absolute, or God] all the essences of things which have been or are still to be are always eternally in act its very essence; just as it is the essence of all, so is it all the essences; . . . it . . . is each of them and none of them in particular." (Cusanus, *Ignorance,* p. 35.) That the soul is "in essence" identical with God, then, in no way "edit[s] out the plural form of 'soul' in Traherne," as Richard Jordan claims in *The Temple of Eternity* (Port Washington, N.Y., 1972), p. 34.

22. Margaret Bottrall, "Traherne's Praise of the Creation," p. 130, writes: "The more we read Traherne, the more we must be struck by his passionate intellectuality. Not things, but thoughts of things are what he values." See also S. L. Bethell, *The Cultural Revolution of the Seventeenth Century* (New York: Roy Publishers, 1951), p. 157; and Itrat-Husain, *The Mystical Element in the Metaphysical Poets of the Seventeenth Century* (Edinburgh: Oliver and Boyd, 1948), p. 298.

23. Sir Thomas Browne, *Religio Medici,* ed. James Winney (Cambridge: At the University Press, 1963), pp. 15–16.

24. Cassirer, *Platonic,* p. 49, makes the point that the Cambridge Platonists held no value higher than contemplation.

25. Fish, *Artifacts,* p. 364.

26. Ibid., p. 371.

27. Ibid., pp. 49–50.

28. Ibid., p. 371.

29. Stewart, *Expanded Voice,* p. 210.

30. Fish, pp. 41–43.

Chapter Three

1. The *Six Days,* as it will usually be referred to for the sake of convenience, has been published in facsimile by George Robert Guffey, ed., *Thomas Traherne: Meditations on the Six Days of the Creation,* The Augustan Reprint Society, No. 119 (Los Angeles: University of California, 1966). All references are to this edition.

2. Wade, *Traherne,* p. 154.

3. "Traherne's debt to Puente's Meditations," *Philological Quarterly* 50 (1971): 163. See also, Catherine A. Owen, "The Authorship of the 'Meditations on the Six Days of Creation' and the 'Meditations and Devotions on the Life of Christ,'" *Modern Language Review* 56 (January 1961): 1–12, and Helen White, *The Metaphysical Poets* (New York: Macmillan, 1936).

4. Sauls, "Debt," p. 163.

5. Ibid., p. 169.

6. As Marks, "Year-Book," p. 31, describes it.

7. Sauls, *"Debt,"* p. 173.

8. Ibid., pp. 161, 162, 163.

9. "Year-Book," p. 35.

10. The manuscript of these meditations, which may be an early draft of the *Centuries,* came to light in 1964 and is to be published as the third volume in the Oxford edition of the works, but their publication has been much delayed, partly by the death of James Osborn, who discovered and was to edit them. For the first notice of their discovery see James Osborn, "A New Traherne Manuscript," *Times Literary Supplement,* October 8, 1964, p. 928.

11. Luis de la Puente, *Meditations upon the Mysteries of our Holie Faith, With the Practice of Mental Prayer Touching the Same,* 2 vols., trans. John Heigham (St. Omers: n.p., 1619), 1: 43.

12. Ibid., 1: 42.

13. Ibid.

14. Arnold Williams, *The Common Expositor: An Account of the Commentaries on Genesis, 1527–1633* (Chapel Hill: University of North Carolina Press, 1948), p. 259.

15. Puente, 2: 708.

16. See Sauls, "Debt," p. 164, n. 8.

17. Puente, 2: 708.

18. As Sauls, "Debt," p. 163, n. 7, points out.

19. Puente, 2: 752.

20. Ibid., 2: 760.

Chapter Four

1. Stewart, *Expanded Voice,* p. 97.

2. *Jerusalem and Albion: The Hebraic Factor in Seventeenth-Century Literature* (New York: Schocken Books 1964), p. 53.

3. For example, Joseph Hall, *Meditations and Vows, Divine and Moral* (1603), in *The Works of the Right Reverend Joseph Hall, D.D.,* 10 vols., new rev. and ed. Philip Wynter (Oxford: At the University Press, 1863), 7: 428,

and Daniel Featley, *Ancilla Pietatis: or, The Hand-Maid to Private Devotion* (London: N. Bourne, 1626), p. 18. Featley could be Traherne's immediate source, but the phrase was probably a commonplace.

4. As Ronald E. McFarland has also pointed out in "Thomas Traherne's *Thanksgivings* . . .," pp. 7–9. McFarland thinks because there is a "summary passage" (p. 7) in the Seventh Thanksgiving, "Thanksgivings for the Wisdom of his WORD," which mentions the subjects of previous Thanksgivings, that "Traherne originally intended it to end the sequence" (p. 7), but he neglects an even more obvious summary of the whole sequence at the beginning of Thanksgiving Eight. Thus, as I point out below, there is more reason to see Thanksgivings One through Eight than One through Seven as constituting a sequence. McFarland's thesis is that in the *Thanksgivings* Traherne "develops a theology of optimism through . . . a religious experience that centers around an active life in this world" and that this makes Traherne's thinking closer "to the Enlightenment than to his own century" (p. 3), but Traherne's theology has essentially nothing to do with "this world" insofar as such a phrase distinguishes a temporal from a nontemporal mode of experience, for even though Traherne understands the fact that experience takes place in a "temporal setting," he does not affirm that experience is necessarily "of this world." Experience takes place *in* the world, but Traherne insisted that it should be apprehended in its eternal, infinite meaning, which is not *of* the world in the sense that "active life in this world" would imply. That Traherne's thinking is optimistic and that this optimism is related to the Restoration and Enlightenment's general trust in man's ability to think things out for himself is true enough, but his thinking affirms the Creation because it perceives the Creation as ultimately spiritual, not the material thing that those who are "of the world" suppose it is. The *Thanksgivings* is, finally, no more optimistic than any other of Traherne's work, and to say that it is "devoted to the affirmation of man's condition in the temporal world" (p. 14) except as man is to understand that world spiritually (the *Centuries* and the *Ethicks* affirm man's condition also) seems either to be in error or to be making a distinction without a difference.

5. *The Poetry of Meditation: A Study in English Literature of the Seventeenth Century* (New Haven: Yale University Press, 1954), p. 38.

6. Puente, *Meditations,* 1: 16.

7. Martz, *Poetry,* p. 37.

8. Puente, 1: 3–4. Quoted by Martz, *Poetry,* pp. 34–35.

9. All quotations of the *Thanksgivings* are from the Margoliouth edition and will be referred to by line number.

10. See above, note 4.

11. "The Language of Vision: Traherne's Cataloguing Style," 94.

12. Ibid., p. 96.

13. *The Private Devotions of Lancelot Andrewes,* trans. F. E. Brightman (London: Methuen and Co., 1903; reprint ed., New York: Meridian Living Age Books, 1961), p. 47.

Chapter Five

1. Margoliouth, 1: xxxviii.

2. Marks, "Year-Book," pp. 60–61.

3. See Stillingfleet, "The Reformation Justified: Preached at Guild-Hall Chapel Septemb. 21. 1673," Sermon 13, in *Works,* 1:192. See note 19, Chapter 1, above.

4. *Roman Forgeries: Or a True Account of False Records Discovering the Impostures and Counterfeit Antiquities of the Church of Rome* (London: 1673). All references to *Forgeries* will be cited in the text as *RF* followed by page number.

5. This approach was given its most famous statement by Hooker, but it was already inherent in Bishop Jewel's methods of debate. See W. M. Southgate, *John Jewel and the Problem of Doctrinal Authority* (Cambridge: Harvard University Press, 1962), pp. 188–91.

6. This position concerning the primitive church was restated many times. Its popularity while Traherne was writing his polemic is attested by an anonymous pamphlet whose title plainly asserts the political implications of Romanism which worried Traherne and others in the Anglican establishment. See *The Religion of the Church of England, the Surest Establishment of the Royal Throne; With the Unreasonable Latitude which the Romanists allow in Point of Obedience to Princes* (London: Randal Taylor and John Williams, 1673), p. 5: "It may well be presumed that in those early dayes of Christianity Religion was in its greatest vigour, and men did not only *best* Know, but Practice what they were obliged to."

7. William Crashaw, *Romish Forgeries and Falsifications: Together with Catholike Restitutions* (London: Matthew Lownes, 1606), sig. E4v.

8. Thomas James, *A Treatise of the Corruption of Scripture, Councels, and Fathers by the Prelates, Pastors, and Pillars of the Church of Rome, for Maintenance of Popery and Irreligion,* in 5 parts (London: Matthew Lownes, 1612), 4:31.

9. See W. K. Jordan, *The Development of Religious Toleration in England;* vol. 1: *From the Beginning of the English Reformation to the Death of Elizabeth;* vol. 2: *From the Accession of James 1 to the Convention of the Long Parliament;* vol. 3: *From the Convention of the Long Parliament to the Restoration;* vol. 4: *Attainment of the Theory and Accomodations in Thought and Institutions;* 4 vols. (Cambridge: Harvard University Press, 1932–1940; reprint ed., Gloucester, Mass.: Peter Smith, 1965), 4:17–19.

10. Crashaw, sig. B4.
11. Crashaw, sigs. C3v and D1.
12. James, 4:9.
13. Ibid., 1: "Dedication."
14. Southgate, p. 132.
15. See above, note 6. Tillotson, Stillingfleet, and Barrow also speak in the same way about the early church.
16. Stewart, *Expanded Voice,* p. 35.
17. See H. Burn-Murdoch, *The Development of the Papacy* (London: Faber and Faber, 1954), pp. 217–18.
18. Ibid., p. 219.
19. Stewart, p. 29; cf. p. 34.

Chapter Six

1. See the indispensable study by Carol Marks Sicherman, "Traherne's Ficino Notebook," pp. 73–81. It is to this article that I am indebted for information about the content and dating of the "Ficino Notebook" and its relation to the *Centuries.*
2. Martz, *Paradise,* pp. 56–57.
3. Gerard H. Cox, III, "Traherne's *Centuries* . . .," p. 23.
4. Jordan, *Temple,* p. 72.
5. Ibid., p. 74.
6. Alexander Ross, *A Centurie of Divine Meditations Upon Predestination, and Its Adjuncts: Wherein are Shewed the Comfortable Uses of this Doctrine* (London: James Young, 1646). Ross's meditations are very short, spare statements of doctrinal points and could harldy have served as a serious model for Traherne.
7. Hall, *Art of Meditation,* in *Works,* 6:49. See note 3, Chapter 4, above.
8. Ibid.
9. Joseph Hall, *Meditations and Vows, Divine and Moral* (1605), in *Works,* 7:443.
10. Ronald E. McFarland, "From Ambiguity to Paradox: Thomas Traherne's 'Things,'" *Wascana Review* 9 (1974): 114–23, discusses the ambiguity that surrounds Traherne's frequent use of *Thing*[*s*] in the poetry, where he sometimes means temporal objects and sometimes "thoughts." McFarland's conclusion is interesting, and it may be that *thing* has a special significance for understanding Traherne's thought, but the ambiguity in his use of the word is not unique; it is consistent with the ambiguities involved in Traherne's use of such other important words as *soul, mind, image,* and *self,* for they all have the same double nature—both finite and infinite—that he sees everywhere.

11. *The Bible as Literature* (New York, 1906), p. 107, quoted by Gay Wilson Allen, *Walt Whitman Handbook* (New York: Hendricks House, 1946), p. 389.

12. Allen, p. 402.

Chapter Seven

1. Osborn, "Manuscript," p. 928.

2. Ibid.

3. Martz, *Paradise,* p. 208.

4. See Osborn, p. 928.

5. Sharon C. Seelig, "The Origins of Ecstasy: Traherne's 'Select Meditations,'" pp. 419–31, has discussed the character of the "Select Meditations" and concluded that in this earlier work Traherne is generally more conservative, more involved with worldly affairs, and less optimistic than in the *Centuries*. She concentrates more than I upon the picture that one gets of Traherne the man and Christian, but her words are, I believe, exactly right and her study the most valuable one at present available. She writes (p. 420): "The persona who emerges is, in comparison to that of *Centuries,* a more traditional, conservative Christian, one more deeply involved in the affairs of the nation and the community, more closely allied to the established Church, more attentive to its ceremonies, doctrines, and benefits."

Chapter Eight

1. Clements, *Mystical Poetry,* p. 5.

2. See Sherrington, *Symbolism.*

3. Only the edition of the poems by Gladys Wade (1932)—which unfortunately does not preserve Thomas's version of individual poems where possible—prints both sequences in full as distinct groups. Margoliouth alters the order of both sequences in order to facilitate comparison between Thomas's and Philip's versions, and Anne Ridler, ed., *Thomas Traherne: Poems, Centuries and Three Thanksgivings* (London, 1966), prints the whole Dobell sequence in its order but only those poems of the Burney sequence that are *not* also included in Dobell. Because it makes at least the whole Dobell group available in its proper order, then, and corrects some errors in Margoliouth's edition, all citations of the poems are from the Ridler edition.

4. Clements, p. 59.

5. See Stewart, *Expanded Voice,* p. 185.

6. Allen, *Whitman,* p. 387.

7. Kenneth Burke, *Counter-Statement* (Los Altos: Hermes Publications, 1953), p. 125.

8. Ibid., p. 126.

9. Allen, *Whitman,* pp. 387–88.

10. Stewart, *Expanded Voice,* pp. 145–55.

11. Quoted from *Songs of Innocence and of Experience Shewing the Two Contrary States of the Human Soul,* A Reproduction of William Blake's Illuminated Book with Introduction and Commentary by Sir Geoffrey Keynes (Paris: Trianon Press, 1967; reprint ed., London: Oxford University Press, 1970), Plate 8.

Selected Bibliography

Primary Sources

1. Published Works

Christian Ethicks. Edited by Carol L. Marks and George R. Guffey. Ithaca: Cornell University Press, 1968.

Meditations on the Six Days of the Creation. Edited with introduction by George R. Guffey. Augustan Reprint Society, No. 119. Los Angeles: Clark Memorial Library, 1966.

The Poetical Works of Thomas Traherne. Edited by Gladys Wade. London: P.J. and A.E. Dobell, 1932; reprint ed., New York: Cooper Square Publishers, 1965.

Roman Forgeries, Or a True Account of False Records Discovering the Impostures and Counterfeit Antiquities of the Church of Rome. By a Faithful Son of the Church of England. London: S. and B. Griffin for Jonathan Edwin, 1673.

Thomas Traherne: Centuries, Poems, and Thanksgivings. Edited by H. M. Margoliouth. 2 vols. Oxford: Clarendon Press, 1958.

Thomas Traherne: Poems, Centuries, and Three Thanksgivings. Edited by Ann Ridler, London: Oxford University Press, 1966.

2. Unpublished Manuscripts

"Early Notebook." (Bodleian Library, Oxford, MS. Lat. misc. f. 45)

"Church's Year Book." (Bodleian Library, Oxford, MS. Eng. th. e. 51)

"Commonplace Book." (Bodleian Library, Oxford, MS. Eng. poet. c. 42)

"Ficino Notebook." (British Museum, London, MS. Burney 126)

"Select Meditations." (Osborn Collecton, Beinecke Library. Yale)

Secondary Sources

1. Biographical and Critical Studies

Clements, A. L. *The Mystical Poetry of Thomas Traherne.* Cambridge: Harvard University Press, 1969. A fine study of the Dobell manuscript poems—their arrangement and language—in the light of the contemplative tradition.

Jordan, Richard Douglas. *The Temple of Eternity: Thomas Traherne's Philosophy of Time.* Port Washington, N. Y.: Kennikat Press, 1972. A worthwhile study of Traherne's concept of "eternity-time," though sometimes making distinctions without differences. Discusses the *Centuries* as patterned upon the Four Estates of man.

Salter, K. W. *Thomas Traherne: Mystic and Poet.* London: Edward Arnold, 1964. An attempt to analyze Traherne's spiritual life with some discussions of his ideas and poetic imagery.

Sherrington, Alison J. *Mystical Symbolism in the Poetry of Thomas Traherne.* St. Lucia, Australia: University of Queensland Press, 1970. An insightful analysis of Traherne's poetic imagery, demonstrating his essentially symbolic technique.

Stewart, Stanley. *The Expanded Voice: The Art of Thomas Traherne.* San Marino, Calif.: Huntington Library, 1970. A very useful discussion of Traherne's characteristic blurring of temporal categories and distinctions through his "rhetoric of erosion." Treats all the works plus manuscripts and proposes a new grouping of the Burney poems by removing all of the Dobell poems from it.

Wade, Gladys. *Thomas Traherne: A Critical Biography.* Princeton: Princeton University Press, 1944. The earliest biography and general study, marred by certain liberties with biographical evidence and an attempt to see into Traherne's soul, but still an important book with valuable information and insights.

2. Bibliographical Studies

Clements, A. L. "Thomas Traherne: A Chronological Bibliography." *Library Chronicle* 35 (1969): 36–51. Nearly complete through 1967.

———. "Addenda to 'Thomas Traherne: A Chronological Bibliography.'" *Library Chronicle* 42, No. 2 (1978): 138–45.

Dees, Jerome S. "Recent Studies in Traherne." *English Literary Renaissance* 4 (1974): 189–96. Succinct and useful, partially annotated bibliography of recent work to 1972.

Guffey, George Robert, ed. *A Concordance to the Poetry of Thomas Traherne.* Berkeley: University of California Press, 1974.

Marks, Carol L. "Thomas Traherne's Commonplace Book." *Papers of the Bibliographical Society of America* 58 (1964): 458–65. A close and valuable examination of Traherne's notes used extensively in the preparation of *Christian Ethicks.*

————. "Thomas Traherne's Early Studies." *Papers of the Bibliographical Society of America* 62 (1968): 511–36. A very important study of Traherne's earliest notebook, providing information about his reading while a student at Oxford.

————. "Traherne's Church Year-Book." *Papers of the Bibliographical Society of America* 60 (1966): 31–72. Indispensable study of a manuscript that provides links between several works and helps date *Roman Forgeries* as a product of the early 1670s not an earlier B.D. thesis as was supposed by Margoliouth.

Osborn, James M. "A New Traherne Manuscript." [London] *Times Literary Supplement,* 8 October 1964, p. 928. A brief announcement and description of the "Select Meditations."

Sauls, [Richard] Lynn. "Traherne's Debt to Puente's *Meditations.*" *Philological Quarterly* 50 (April 1971): 161–74. Describes significant discovery of Traherne's dependence upon Puente's work for the *Meditations on the Six Days of the Creation.*

Sicherman, Carol Marks. "Traherne's Ficino Notebook." *Papers of the Bibliographical Society of America* 63 (1969): 73–81. Important description of Traherne's studies in Renaissance Platonism in late 1660s.

3. Shorter Critical Studies

Bottrall, Margaret. "Traherne's Praise of Creation." *Critical Quarterly* 1 (Summer 1959): 126–33. Studies Traherne's spiritual imagination and explains his preference for thoughts over things.

Colie, Rosalie L. "Thomas Traherne and the Infinite: The Ethical Compromise." *Huntington Library Quarterly* 21 (November 1957): 69–82. A clear explanation of some of Traherne's most important ideas, emphasizing his insistence upon knowledge of the infinite as the means of salvation.

Cox, Gerard H., III. "Traherne's *Centuries*: A Platonic Devotion of 'Divine Philosophy.'" *Modern Philology* 69 (August 1971): 10–24. Sees the structure of the *Centuries* in Traherne's Platonic principles, and suggests an order based upon God's laws, works, and the self, concluding that the work is "an interesting failure."

Day, Malcolm M. "'Naked Truth' and the Language of Thomas Traherne." *Studies in Philology* 68 (July 1971): 305–25. Discusses Traherne's use of abstraction and paradox as a means of bringing his reader to a perception of God.

————. "Traherne and the Doctrine of Pre-existence." *Studies in Philology* 65 (January 1968): 81–97. Argues that Traherne's mystical view includes a doctrine of the pre-existence of the impersonal, infinite-eternal soul.

Goldknopf, David. "The Disintegration of Symbol in a Meditative Poet." *College English* 30 (October 1968): 48–59. Discusses the problem of poetic imagery in Traherne's Neoplatonic perspective, which inherently disparages the senses.

Grant, Patrick. *The Transformation of Sin: Studies in Donne, Herbert, Vaughan, and Traherne.* Montreal: McGill-Queens University Press, 1974. An excellent study of Traherne's work against the contrast between an Augustinian "guilt" and an "enlightenment" culture. Sees Traherne in the light of the pre-Nicene St. Irenaeus's theology.

Jennings, Elizabeth. "The Accessible Art: A Study of Thomas Traherne's *Centuries of Meditations." Twentieth Century* 167 (February 1960): 140–51. The *Centuries* as an example of "the art of sharing."

King, Francis. "Thomas Traherne: Intellect and Felicity." In *Restoration Literature: Critical Approaches,* pp. 121–43. Edited by Harold Love. London: Methuen, 1972. Correctly sees that Traherne writes from the perspective of "realization" rather than search, but regards this perspective as facilely adopted by Traherne.

Leishman, James Blair. *The Metaphysical Poets: Donne, Herbert, Vaughan, Traherne.* Oxford: Clarendon Press, 1934. A good early study of Traherne's place in the metaphysical poetic tradition.

McFarland, Ronald E. "From Ambiguity to Paradox: Thomas Traherne's 'Things.'" *Wascana Review* 9 (1974): 114–23. Provides insight into Traherne's use of a "neutral" word to suggest an important point of philosophical discrimination.

————. "Thomas Traherne's *Thanksgivings* and the Theology of Optimism." *Enlightenment Essays* 4, No. 2 (Spring 1973): 3–14. An interesting study that points out the sequential nature of the *Thanksgivings* but claims a special importance of the work for Traherne's optimistic viewpoint.

Marks, Carol L. "Thomas Traherne and Cambridge Platonism." *Publications of the Modern Language Association* 81 (December 1966): 521–34. The best short analysis of the relationship of Traherne's thought to the ideas of the Cambridge Platonists.

————. "Thomas Traherne and Hermes Trismegistus." *Renaissance News* 19 (1966): 118–31. Discusses Traherne's fascination with the philosophy of Hermes, arguing that Hermes provided affirmation of Traherne's own thinking.

Martz, Louis L. *The Paradise Within: Studies in Vaughan, Traherne, and Milton.* New Haven: Yale University Press, 1964. An important study of the *Centuries* in the Augustinian-Bonaventuran tradition of meditation. Sensitive and illuminating, although the thesis is somewhat misleading.

Ridlon, Harold G. "The Function of the 'Infant-Ey' in Traherne's Poetry."
   Studies in Philology 61 (1964): 627–39. Traherne's concept of infancy and
   childhood as a key to his theme of man's relation to God and the world.
Sandbank, S. "Thomas Traherne on the Place of Man in the Universe." In
   Studies in English Language and Literature, edited by Alice Shalvi and A.
   A. Mendilow, pp. 121–36. *Scripta Hierosolymitana: Publications of the
   Hebrew University,* vol. 17. Jerusalem: Magnes Press, 1966. One of the
   most intelligent and perceptive analyses of Traherne's efforts to
   "spiritualize" everything and affirm the dignity of man.
Seelig, Sharon C. "The Origins of Ecstasy: Traherne's 'Select Meditations.'"
   English Literary Renaissance 9 (1979): 419–31. A valuable commentary
   upon the still unpublished and unstudied meditations found by
   Osborn.
Selkin, Carl M. "The Language of Vision: Traherne's Cataloguing Style."
   English Literary Renaissance 6 (1976): 92–104. An analysis of Traherne's
   use of catalogues. Suggests that catalogues are a unitive, nonlinear
   language directly expressing a "deep level" vision of the oneness of all in
   God.
Trimpey, John E. "An Analysis of Traherne's 'Thoughts I.'" *Studies in
   Philology* 68 (1971): 88–104. Interesting discussion of Traherne's intel-
   lectual, "logical" mysticism by an examination of his assertions in one
   of the poems.
Uphaus, Robert. "Thomas Traherne: Perception as Process." *University of
   Windsor Review* 3 (Spring 1968): 19–27. Discusses the difference be-
   tween "bare perception" and "apprehension" in Traherne's philosophy
   of apostasy and redemption.
Wallace, John Malcolm. "Thomas Traherne and the Structure of Medita-
   tion." *English Literary History* 25 (June 1958): 78–89. Claims that the
   Dobell sequence constitutes a complete five-part Ignatian meditation.
Webber, Joan. *The Eloquent "I": Style and Self in SeventeenthCentury Prose.*
   Madison: University of Wisconsin Press, 1968. Contains a valuable
   chapter on Traherne's merging of self and audience into a spiritual
   community through a typical use of rhetorical patterns.
Williams, Melvin G. "Thomas Traherne: Center of God's Wealth." *Cithara*
   3 (1963): 32–40. Discusses Traherne's presumed self-centered
   Christianity.

Index

6

Colleges Unite to Save Minds

Client: United Negro College Fund
Agency: Young and Rubicam
New York
Target: Potential donors (all ethnic backgrounds)

One of the most successful public service campaigns ever was created for an ethnic client by a nonminority advertising agency. Young and Rubicam has effectively handled the United Negro College Fund advertising campaign since 1972.

The purpose of studying this case is to provide students with a look at how nonminorities can and do create effective advertising featuring ethnic issues, products, or services. This case also represents the durability of good concept and execution in marketing to any audience and clearly demonstrates how a campaign about and featuring minorities can have appeal to nonminorities as well.

At the end of this case, students should be able to do the following:

1. Recognize that good advertising is an extremely effective tool with any audience
2. Understand the principles of public service campaigns aimed at ethnic audiences
3. Understand how proper research into the target audience can assist any agency in developing minority campaigns

⮞ Profile of the Organization

The United Negro College Fund (UNCF) was started in 1944 by Dr. Frederick D. Patterson, the third president of Tuskegee Institute. He began the Fund as a response to waning public support for black colleges in the early 1940s. It was Dr. Patterson's belief that black colleges should unite in search of funds rather than to pursue financial assistance on their own.[1]

Twenty-seven schools joined the Fund, and a number of prominent Americans gave their support to the organization. President Franklin Roosevelt backed the program, as did John D. Rockefeller, Jr., who chaired the Fund's National Advisory Committee. Winthrop W. Aldrich, chairman of the board of the Chase National Bank (now Chase Manhattan), served as UNCF's first treasurer, and Walter Hoving, president of Lord and Taylor, was the organization's first national campaign chairman. The first campaign was a major success, raising $765,000.[2]

In 1951, the Fund launched the National Mobilization of Resources for the United Negro Colleges campaign. John D. Rockefeller donated securities valued at approximately $5 million to start UNCF's first capital campaign. UNCF raised over $14.6 million by 1957 for capital improvements for its member colleges and universities.[3]

UNCF has faced a number of challenges throughout its history. Following the 1954 *Brown v. Topeka Board of Education* landmark desegregation decision, the value of the Fund's existence was questioned. Some believed that if black students could have access to white institutions, they would no longer need black colleges. The Fund responded by saying that desegregation would not take place immediately. Therefore, black students would still need a place to receive an education.

During the 1960s, the Fund was confronted with the issues of the civil rights movement. Its students and alumni participated in protests and rallies, but many donors were reluctant to give money to schools involved in the struggle. UNCF survived this turbulent period and managed to maintain its funding support throughout the decade.

In 1972, the Advertising Council accepted UNCF as a public service campaign. The Fund's third capital campaign, the Capital Resources Development Program, was launched in 1978. The two-year effort raised over $60 million.[4] Since 1980, the Fund has sponsored the annual "Lou Rawls Parade of Stars" telethon. In 1991, Congressman William H. Gray III became the Fund's eighth chief executive officer.

What the United Negro College Fund Wanted to Accomplish

In 1971, UNCF was relatively unknown to American audiences. The Fund had a core group of staunch supporters, but among the working class, there was little understanding of how the organization functioned. It was at that time that the Fund's executive director, Vernon Jordan, approached Young and Rubicam Advertising about developing an image and campaign strategy for the organization. The Fund wanted a campaign that accomplished several goals simultaneously. Young and Rubicam's role was to create public awareness of the Fund and thus a favorable climate toward the Fund's goals. The overall objective was to predispose individuals, groups, corporations, and foundations to contribute money.

Other goals included creating awareness among prospective donors that UNCF helps financially disadvantaged students receive a quality education. The campaign also needed to overcome a lingering though faulty perception that blacks had "made it." During the early 1970s, African Americans began appearing in larger numbers than before on television and in feature films. More than ever were attending college, but the numbers were still well below the national average.

Concept/Theme Development

Research indicated that donors and prospective donors were 60 percent white and 40 percent black; were above age 45; and, generally had middle-class incomes. They would give money to causes in which they had a personal conviction, and they tended to respond better to emotional appeals supported by rational appeals than to rational appeals alone.

To reach and affect the target audience, a campaign would need to reach the audience at several levels. First, it would need to appeal to them on an emotional level. They would need to care about the students who could not receive an adequate education because of a lack of money. Once the target audience was interested in the people being affected, the rational, intellectual appeal was presented to support their feelings.

The agency developed the themeline "A Mind Is a Terrible Thing to Waste" to accomplish both emotional and intellectual goals. The themeline could hardly be perceived as offensive to any audience, despite their educational level or ethnicity. The concept of waste was one that was clear to the entire target audience. Resources, in this case human minds, were being squandered. It was clearly an intellectual argument with which people could identify. Those feelings could be translated into a tangible action, that is, giving money.

Execution

Since 1972, a number of creative executions have been used for the UNCF campaign. The campaign has evolved over time, moving from one central idea to another designed to reflect the interests and concerns of audiences during particular time periods.

The first commercial, entitled "Disappearing Mind," aired in 1971. It focused on the ways in which all of society suffers because some are denied an education. In 1974, an ad debuted featuring a black mother working as a cleaning woman to help pay for her child's education. Some criticized the portrayal of the cleaning woman as stereotypical.

During the mid-1970s, the agency produced commercials with a strong historical theme. It used slavery, plantation images, and chains to evoke strong emotional responses from audiences. During this same time period, the television epic "Roots" was first aired. The unpleasantness of slavery was used as a reminder of the long-term struggle of black people in America. In the spot called "The Bodie Plantation," it was clearly demonstrated how blacks were forbidden to read. The implication was that making reading legal did not provide access to education for African Americans; many were still denied a chance because of lack of money.

In 1976, the campaign was set to the music of Ray Charles, who extended the theme with an original score. A memorable line from this spot was "We're not asking for a handout, just a hand." Opera diva Leontyne Price sang the song again in 1984.

By the beginning of the 1980s, the spots moved away from the heavy emotional appeals centering around slavery and suffering and toward a more positive approach. The new breed of UNCF commercials showed UNCF graduates in professional settings. The change coincided with the start of the Reagan years, in which the notion of pulling oneself up by the bootstraps was popular. Americans had grown weary of hearing about welfare, affirmative action, and racism, and preferred to focus on the perception that any American could make it if given the chance.

During the mid-1980s and beyond, the campaign returned to the concept of how the individual suffers without the money to attend college. These ads showed smart students with the desire, but without the resources, to continue their education. It played up the disappointment of their families.

According to Young and Rubicam, one of the most successful of its UNCF commercials was the "Little Brother" spot, aired in 1987 and 1988. The ad showed a young man being told by his parents that they are unable to send him to college. His younger brother offers the money in his piggy bank as assistance. The success of the spot was measured in the number of times it ran. It aired more times in its 60-second format than in its 30-second form. Donated media time for the spot totaled over $40 million, and donations to the UNCF increased almost 20 percent in one year.

The agency's 1991–1992 campaign, "Graduation," shows a high school commencement ceremony in which students are discussing their future plans. When asked what he plans to do in the upcoming fall, one student must tell his classmates that he'll being staying home because he has no money for college. This campaign is the result of research indicating that the need for UNCF was more urgent than ever before. This campaign was supported with consumer print ads, billboards, and business press advertisements expressing the need for continued support for UNCF.

Conclusion

As a result of Young and Rubicam's UNCF campaign, contributions to the Fund rose significantly. The campaign's themeline, "A Mind Is a Terrible Thing to Waste," is one of the most memorable ever to emerge from a public service campaign.

The UNCF campaign was successful from a number of perspectives. First, the commercials accomplished what the Fund wanted, that is, awareness and donations. Next, the campaign had crossover appeal; no segment of the population is alienated from the message. The attractiveness of the spots made them interesting to watch. Finally, the UNCF campaign was useful in getting many black college-aged students to appreciate the value of an education. The historical struggle and the modern-day challenge of getting an education were clearly brought to light by the Fund's advertisements.

"A Mind Is a Terrible Thing to Waste" has become the identifying theme of UNCF. However, not everyone has found the slogan to be memorable. In a speech that members of the Fund would like to forget, former Vice President Dan Quayle misquoted the line when he said, "It is a terrible thing to lose one's mind."

DISCUSSION QUESTIONS ◄-----------------------------

1. What basic elements make this campaign a success?
2. What distinguishes this campaign from other public service campaigns?
3. Should UNCF have used a minority advertising agency?
4. How can other schools trying to attract minorities use the principles employed in the campaign?

Endnotes

1. *A Brief History of the United Negro College Fund* (New York: UNCF, 1993), 1–8.
2. Ibid.
3. Ibid.
4. Ibid.

VIEW FROM THE TOP

Valerie Graves ◄-----------------------------
Senior Vice President/Creative Director
UniWorld

Valerie Graves is an advertising veteran. Before being named senior vice president/creative director for UniWorld, she was an award-winning associate creative director for Ross Roy, Inc., and a senior copywriter at J. Walter Thompson; Kenyon and Eckhardt; Batten, Barten, Durstine, and Osborn, Inc. (BBDO); and D'Arcy MacManus Massius. She has worked on major accounts, including Nestea, Kmart, Ocean Spray, Timex, and Dodge Cars and Trucks. A native of Pontiac, Michigan, she attended Wayne State University in Detroit and studied filmmaking at New York University.

Advertising Age selected Graves as one of the "Best and Brightest People in Advertising." She has received a number of CEBA awards as well as awards from the Art Director's Club of New York, the Boston Advertising Club, and the Maine Advertising Club.

In 1992, she worked on Bill Clinton's presidential campaign.

How are African American woman portrayed in advertising?

We are not often portrayed in advertising if you look at advertising as a whole. In general, when we are portrayed, we are depicted in archetypal roles. We are shown as mothers, housewives, or occasionally as glamorous women, depending on the product. I don't think we are portrayed any differently from other women. But I do think we are not shown very often.

What changes have you seen in ethnic advertising in the past 19 years?

I see a shift, but not quite enough of one. I see ethnic advertising as something that in the past had to be done as either a preventive measure or a reality for solving problems that companies had in dealing with the audience. A slight change in the perception of us is that now we are a consumer force and advertising is an opportunity rather than a way to solve a problem.

Are African American women represented well in the advertising industry?

No!

Are there any advertising themes using women you find offensive?

I find sexually explicit ads offensive. I can't figure out why the press is so silent about this. Another ad I find offensive is the one that says women base their selection of fashionable shoes on a favored, time-honored method—mood swings. This sort of hormone-oriented headline gets on my nerves.

What do you suggest to improve the image of women in advertising?

I think that advertising in general tends to objectify everyone, not just women. If we could just find a way to put more image truth into advertising. I do feel that there is a certain core of meaning missing in advertising. This is not in ethnic terms, but it does seem like what a colleague of mine said: "Advertising no longer has a soul."

How do you find an African American agency different from a mainstream agency?

As a creative person in an African American agency, you get a lot more respect. Right from the beginning you are considered to be a person of intelligence and certain capabilities. You have been hired, and you don't have to prove yourself constantly. It's assumed that you know what you are doing. Also, because many of us are from the same cultural background, we don't find ourselves talking across cultural lines and concerned about each other's perceptions, trying to figure out each other's political, cultural, and racial positions before we talk.

What is the most difficult aspect for a minority agency competing for advertising accounts?

There is a perception somewhere that black agencies have to do more for fewer dollars and that we are deserving of fewer dollars. We are expected to execute production and everything else at the same level as a general market agency while at the same time charging less for our services. You have to be strong to withstand the unfairness of working at a minority agency or being a minority agency.

How do you think advertising could improve the image of minorities in this society?

Things happen all the time in this country, and people say that it wasn't a racial incident. The whole country is in a state of denial. The issue cannot be dealt with unless people face it. As long as there is denial the real and true racism in this country cannot come out. The media have a lot more to do in changing the perception of minorities than advertising does.

What advice would you give minority students pursuing a career in advertising?

Do it. There's a lot of opportunity in the advertising industry. It's a fun business. It's a wonderful way to learn about film. It's lucrative and underdeveloped, and this may not be a bad time to break in. On the creative side, it's a talent-based industry. You have to be aggressive and persistent to find a good job. That goes for people of any race. A few years ago when we had a program to try to recruit minority copywriters, we opened it to everyone. Most of the efforts were inferior to general market efforts. I was disappointed in them, and I told these young people that I was going to tell them the truth about the problems in their work. I told them to make the improvements and come back and see me again. Almost none of them did. Maybe one. I hope that students come prepared for true challenges.

What are the main problems you have been faced with while working in a male-dominated business?

You have to demand respect. You have to make a noise to even be noticed. There is a romanticism with young, white males in the business. A good example would be the case of a white male working on the Clinton campaign who essentially took credit for the work everyone else did. The trade press covered the story, but the mainstream media was very willing to accept the fact that it was this white man who had done all the work, even though the *New York Times* and the *Washington Post* reported whom Clinton and Gore had selected to be on their advertising team. The press didn't do any research at all. They just accepted that this "golden boy" had done it all.

Can you talk a bit about your experience with the Clinton campaign?

I was not recruited for minority-targeted work. My presence on the team might have been the result of a letter from an African American advertising executive that said the African American community should be represented on the team. I don't know if it was something they were considering in the first place or whether it was in response to the letter. Diversity is something President Clinton is very sincere about.

What was your role?

I was a creative and media consultant to both the Clinton–Gore campaign and the Democratic National Committee. On the latter, I did do advertising targeted to minorities, created specifically to run on BET (Black Entertainment Network) and on radio, featuring Magic Johnson. When they decided to do targeted communication, it was just natural that they selected me to do that. I wrote advertising, provided creative direction, and hired and contracted people to produce the commercials.

How did the Clinton campaign target minority audiences?

They didn't. The only thing was a radio spot of Magic Johnson endorsing Clinton. That ran on black-formatted radio stations. It was indicative of Clinton to speak to general audiences and not pick out specific groups. The Democratic party, on the other hand, did more targeted advertising.

If you were to work on Clinton's campaign again, what would you do differently?

Of the three commercials I presented, two were produced. The one that was not selected featured an inner-city black kid. It was based on something Clinton said on the "Arsenio Hall Show" (during the campaign). Tell kids "Stay in school and study and stay out of trouble and you will be able to go to college and get a good job. You won't make as much as a drug dealer, but you will be a respectable citizen." I would make more commercials with simple, true messages like this.

Honda Strikes a Chord with Black College Students

Client: American Honda
Agency: Muse Cordero Chen
Los Angeles
Target: Historically black colleges and universities

This case is an example of how a special event can be used as a marketing tool. It shows how a major event can be created and how publicity and excitement can be generated. Further, this case looks at how advertising can be used to promote an event effectively. It also discusses how collateral materials can be developed to support a special program and how a company can use an event to position itself favorably among a specified target audience.

At the end of this case, students should be able to do the following:

1. Recognize how special events are created to meet particular goals
2. Understand an advertising agency's role in developing a special program
3. Identify some of the elements that make a special event effective

Profile of the Company

American Honda was established in 1959 as a subsidiary of Honda Motor Company Limited. At the time, the Japanese-based company was better known in America as a motorcycle producer than an auto manufacturer. By the beginning of the 1960s, Honda was the world's largest motorcycle company, with sales of $55 million.[1] It was not until 1967 that Honda began making trucks and cars. The company expanded its product line to include lawn mowers, outboard motors, tillers, and generators. It took six years for Honda cars to catch on in America. The successful introduction of the economical Honda Civic in 1973 was aided by a worldwide oil crisis. Since that time, Honda has been a dominant force in American automobile sales. The Honda Accord was the best-selling car in America for four straight years, from 1989 to 1992. Honda sales topped $14.7 billion in 1991.[2]

Having an American subsidiary has helped Honda gain acceptance in the United States. When social pressure came down on foreign automakers for allegedly stealing American jobs, Honda responded by pointing to its Ohio manufacturing facility. Americans who purchase Hondas made at the Ohio plant are told that they are not really buying a Japanese product, but an American-built automobile instead.

What American Honda Wanted to Accomplish

American Honda wanted to demonstrate its commitment to the historically black colleges and universities (HBCUs). In addition, the company wanted to capture a leadership position for itself by acknowledging the intelligence and competitive spirit of black college students. Black college students were an ideal target audience for an auto manufacturer because they are likely to purchase automobiles when they complete their educations.

American Honda wanted black colleges to know that it was supportive of their mission. The corporation wanted black students to recognize that it respected and appreciated their knowledge and was willing to showcase it. Unlike the work done by the United Negro College Fund, American Honda was not simply making a donation to the cause of African American education. The company wanted students themselves to raise the money. It was simply providing a vehicle through which this goal could be accomplished.

Concept/Theme Development

The advertising agency of Muse Cordero Chen conducted 16 focus groups for American Honda in a number of major cities, including New York, Los Angeles, Philadelphia, St. Louis, Memphis, Chicago, and Atlanta. The research was designed to uncover attitudes about the corporation and about issues facing the black American community.

Major problems identified included illegal drug consumption and the erosion of the black man and the family unit. The agency found that African Americans wanted companies to be more responsive to the needs of the community, specifically in the area of education. Therefore, education was chosen as the key element in any advertising or public relations campaign aimed at this target audience. The agency developed the American Honda Campus All-Star Challenge to meet this need. The event was a mix of old and new. The idea of a college bowl was popularized in the 1960s. Students from different academic institutions were tested on their knowledge of a wide variety of subjects.

In the 1991 American Honda Campus All-Star Challenge, students from HBCUs competed against each other in the same format. The schools received grants for their success, with the grand-prize-winning school earning an award of $50,000 and the right to call itself the National Champion.

From its inception, the Campus All-Star Challenge was designed to be more than just a contest. It was created to spark enthusiasm and excitement on campuses across the country. Schools needed to identify their best students and prepare them for the event. Teams needed to work together and study the material they thought would be covered. Schools received $1,000 for playing and $5,000 if they advanced to the televised round.

In a modified version of basketball's NCAA tournament, 64 teams began the contest. Sectional playoffs were sponsored in four different geographical regions of the country. Each was hosted by an HBCU. At the sectionals, each team played seven preliminary matches, for a total of 28 games. The event continued until four final teams emerged to advance to the National Championship Round, which was televised on BET (Black Entertainment Network).

The sectional playoffs were also designed to provide students with an opportunity to meet alumni from HBCUs. There was an opening dinner at each round with a guest speaker.

The monetary awards, provided by American Honda, totaled over $305,000. The company stipulated that the grants were to be used to upgrade and retrofit campus facilities, libraries, and archives or to provide for institutional research.

Execution

Muse Cordero Chen created a number of advertisements and collateral pieces to accompany the Campus All-Star Challenge campaign. The four-color magazine ads featured real students in search of an education. One headline read, "Before Jacqueline Gill can direct her first film, she needs a good location." The copy discussed the need for a school to have a film department that is well-equipped, which takes money. It further stated that the Honda Campus All-Star Challenge was helping schools like the one Jacqueline attends earn money for such equipment. The bold and dramatic visuals feature filmmaking paraphernalia, such as a stopwatch and reels of celluloid. A smaller picture of the student is shown, with a one-sentence identification underneath.

A similar ad shows a medical student, with the headline "In order for Marvin Young to attend medical school, he needs an operation." From the headline, the copy picks up on the word "operation" and explains it more thoroughly as an "...educational operation. One with books. Labs. Equipment for the labs..."

Another series of print advertisements used one graphic and a one-sentence headline designed to pique the reader's curiosity: for example, "How fly fishing can save a teacher's job." To find the answer to this intriguing statement, the reader must move on to the body copy, which begins with the question "Just what does fly fishing have to do with saving a teacher's job? you might ask." The answer to the question is then provided: "Well, plenty." The copy further explains the All-Star Challenge in detail. Other ads in the series featured the headlines "How mussels can support a medical department" and "How a football team can survive on peanuts."

Attractive visuals were selected to stand alone at the center of each advertisement. Colorful fishing flies, perfectly formed peanuts, and slimy mussels all float in a borderless design above the bold headline. The familiar Honda logo appears only at the bottom right-hand corner of the ads.

Other collateral material included a black and white poster for campus distribution. The headline read, "We're looking for a few smart alecks, wise guys, and know-it-alls." The body copy was aimed directly at students, with lines like, "The students we're looking for here think it's far more important to make the Dean's List than the party list." There was even a "Know-It-All" newsletter with articles ranging from how teams compete, to a question-and-answer section on rules and procedures for the games.

Courtesy Muse Cordero Chen, Inc.

Conclusion

The American Honda College All-Star Challenge effectively used a combination of advertising, publicity, and special events marketing techniques to send a message to the target audience. It was a win–win campaign. The contest generated positive publicity for the corporation, while also raising money for the schools.

Muse Cordero Chen accomplished a number of goals for American Honda through this special event. The event helped to create awareness of the company as an entity beyond that of car and motorcycle maker. Because African Americans were rarely, if ever, allowed to compete in college bowls during the 1960s and 1970s, this was the first opportunity for students to display their academic talents publicly. In addition, televising the finals on BET was a coup because a large number of viewers in the target audience could see the event.

DISCUSSION QUESTIONS

1. While demonstrating its commitment to HBCUs does American Honda run the risk of alienating or ignoring the large number of African American students enrolled at predominantly white colleges?
2. If so, what type of program could the company design for black students at white colleges?
3. What would you do to extend the life of this event?

Endnotes

1. Honda Motor Company Limited, *International Directory of Company Histories,* vol. 1 (Chicago: St. James Press, 1988), 174–176.
2. Honda Motor Company Limited, *Moody's Handbook of Common Stocks* (New York: Moody's Investors Service, Inc., 1993).

VIEW FROM THE TOP

J. Melvin Muse
Chairman
Muse Cordero Chen

J. Melvin Muse's advertising and public relations career began in 1972. With a degree in advertising from Michigan State University, Muse went to work as public relations manager for Olin Corporation in Connecticut. He later worked for Reid Advertising, Hubbert Advertising, Costa Mesa, and Rogers and French & Company. He founded J. Melvin Muse & Co. in 1984. Two years later, the company merged with Mavis Cordero and David Chen to form Muse Cordero Chen, Inc., billed as the nation's only multicultural advertising agency.

The firm develops communications programs targeting consumers of African, Asian, and Hispanic descent. Major clients include American Honda, the California Department of Conservation, Nike, and Home Savings of America. In 1986, billings were reported at $2.5 million; by 1990, billings had reached $20 million.

Muse is active in the American Association of Advertising Agencies, the Los Angeles Creative Club, and the Western States Advertising Agency Association.

Is your agency a minority firm or a multicultural firm?

Muse Cordero Chen breaks the box of what a minority agency is. Our very existence is a large feat. We are stepping up to just being an ad agency, as opposed to an ethnic advertising agency. We've gotten more general market reviews in the last three months than in the last five years. We lost them all, but you can't win unless you play.

Outside of getting more business, what are you trying to accomplish?

We're up to changing the face of the business by reinventing it. We're reshaping how advertising is done. We are not trying to be something we are not. All we really want to be is an advertising agency that is productive and vital and does great work.

The idea of a multicultural advertising agency makes a lot of sense. But how does being multicultural affect the way you do business?

Diversity is our "secret weapon." I believe that diversity of culture adds a brilliant creative spark to idea development, and that means better work. Different perspectives generate something extraordinary. Without diversity, all work would look the same. We're showing how diversity can give work better value.

Why do you think this model is effective?

This agency is a product of the times. We are pioneering something that is trying to happen for the ad industry as a whole. This rock of separatism is massive. We haven't broken the rock down, but we're trying. Maybe in 10 years multiculturalism in advertising agencies will be the norm, not the exception.

What problems do you face as a multicultural advertising firm?

We are constantly confronting perceptions. The challenge is to be perceived the way you really are and not the way others would have you be. Perception is all you have in the advertising business. Some people think that because we are not Anglos, we can't be brilliant ad pros. That's ridiculous.

What is the role of multiculturalism in creating advertising?

We find that one of the things that has an impact on culture—excuse me, I said it wrong—one of the things that has an impact on perspective is the notion of culture. This includes how one grows up in life, what one learns, and how one views one's environment. Those cultural distinctions have a great deal to do with forming culture, and they have an interesting pull on our perspective. It is that perspective that people bring or don't bring to advertising.

What's in the future for Muse Cordero Chen?

Right now, we do the kind of business we do out of necessity. It's like the old Negro Baseball League. The athletes played to black audiences because they couldn't get on white teams. We want to break the back of that mentality. All I want is an opportunity to compete on a world-class basis. I love winning and hate losing. If this agency and I are to achieve, we must keep moving toward that goal. In time, it will happen. And when it does, it will transform the ad business. Bet on it!

Liquor Company Closes the Gap Between East and West

8

Client: Remy Martin
Agency: L³
         New York
Target: Asian Americans

This case looks at how advertising and marketing efforts can influence the consumer behavior of target audiences. It also examines the critical role of culture in developing and executing advertising aimed at a specific ethnic group. The case deals with nuances of an immigrant community, including the perceptions they bring to the purchase of a product.

At the end of this case, students should be able to do the following:

1. Understand how traditional and archetypal images can be used to reach ethnic audiences
2. Discuss the role of price in positioning and marketing a product to an ethnic audience
3. Analyze how the approach taken by an ethnic advertising agency is different from that of a general market firm

Profile of the Company

Remy Martin Amerique, Inc., is a wholly owned subsidiary of the E. Remy Martin Champaigne Company of Cognac, France. The company is responsible for U.S. distribution of the high-priced imported brandy. Remy Martin of France employed 600 people and reported worldwide sales of $220 million in 1989.[1] With 13 percent of the U.S. cognac market, Remy Martin is in fourth place. The market leader is Hennessy, holding 39 percent of the cognac drinkers. Courvoisier and Martell are in second and third place.[2]

What is perhaps most interesting about Remy Martin cognac is the mystique surrounding the product and the entire cognac category. In a 1986 article, *Bon Appétit* magazine called cognac the "world's greatest brandy."[3] Cognac's reputation is a result of the laborious and lengthy process required to produce it. Most cognac is made in France, even though the word *brandy* comes from the Dutch word *brandewijn*, which means "burnt wine."

Cognac can be grown only under special conditions. Sandy soil is required for the grapes. The wine derived from the grapes must be distilled twice. After distillation, the brandy is stored in small barrels made of special oak to reduce the possibility of bitterness. After at least one and a half years, the "youngest" brandies are sold. However, according to cognac experts, the longer the aging process, the smoother the taste.[4]

How much cognac costs is a direct result of the aging process. Cognac aged for three to five years is called VS or Very Superior. VSOP (Very Special Old Pale) is the labeling given to cognac stored for at least four years. By law, XO (Extra Old) cognac must be aged no less than five and a half years. Cognac in this category can be aged for between 15 and 25 years. The top of the line in cognacs are the Grand Reserves. Many of these are 50 years old. Remy Martin's contribution to this category is called Louis XIII, which can sell for upward of $1,000 per bottle.

Remy Martin's cognac sales are concentrated in the VSOP category. It controls 70 percent of the U.S. market for high-end cognac.[5] In 1992, Remy earned $125 million on cognac sales, about 25 percent of total U.S. sales.[6] These numbers represent a decline in cognac sales that began in the 1980s. Cognac marketers attribute the flat sales to a decrease in overall alcohol consumption and a stuffiness associated with the product. Many long-time cognac drinkers were growing older, and some younger consumers found that an after-dinner drink did not mix with their lifestyles.

What Remy Martin Wanted to Accomplish

In Asian communities, there are many reasons to celebrate. Asians tend to celebrate major accomplishments, births, and a host of holidays. As with other populations, alcoholic beverages are often a part of the festivities. Cognac, in particular, is a very popular drink in Hong Kong, though it is served differently in Asia than in America. In the United States, cognac is traditionally considered an after-dinner liquor. In China, it is drunk more like wine. It is consumed more heavily and in a wide variety of settings and times. About 3 percent of the general population drinks cognac; Asian consumption is much higher.

Remy Martin wanted to transfer the popularity of cognac in China to Asian immigrants in America. The company wanted to extend the use of the brand by giving consumers more reasons and opportunities to purchase it. Remy also wanted to take advantage of Asian immigrants' strong belief in their cultural values and traditions. Instead of opting for the American tradition of using champagne as the drink of choice for celebrations, the Asian community could maintain some of its heritage by drinking cognac.

Remy Martin's goal was also to dethrone Johnny Walker Red, a popular drink in the Asian American community. Part of Johnny Walker's success was believed to come from the fact that the color red is good luck in Chinese culture. The cognac manufacturer wanted to increase sales in the Asian American community, but to do it in a manner that would blend well with existing Chinese values and behaviors.

Concept/Theme Development

L^3 approached the Remy Martin campaign with a clear understanding of what needed to be accomplished. The advertising would need to be distinctly Asian in orientation, concept, and execution. There was no need to create awareness of the brand with the audience; they were already familiar with it. Likewise, there was no need to educate consumers about product usage. What L^3 set out to do was to let Asian consumers know that they could use the brand as they used it in their homeland. Further, they could use the brand for new and different reasons from those to which they had become accustomed.

In developing the concept for Remy Martin Cognac, L³ also considered the price of the brand. At the high end, the product ranged from $80 to $110 per bottle, making it a special occasion drink. Inherent in the price was also the product's prestige.

The overall goal of the advertising was to blend the cultures of Asia and America in a manner that was palatable to Asian consumers. Any suggestion that they should forfeit their culture for purely American values would be unacceptable, as might be a message that would ignore the fact that they were now living in another land. To be successful, the concept would need to address both cultures in a sensitive and meaningful manner.

Execution

L³ designed a print campaign for the XO superpremium brand that expressed three different concepts. The first was celebration, a notion easily accepted and embraced by the target audience. From Chinese New Year, to graduations, to acceptance into college, Asian communities celebrate special occasions openly and with considerable fanfare.

The second concept involved the idea of gift giving. Asians tend to give presents to those they like and enjoy. Gifts are clear demonstrations of affection and respect. For those who had not considered the gift of cognac, the ad made it clear that this was an acceptable and desirable choice.

Banquet celebration was the third concept executed for the campaign. Remy wanted consumers to include its product at their banquet celebrations. The themeline for each of the ads was "Remy shares all your happy moments."

As important as the execution of the concept was placement of the ads. Obviously, they would need to be in media that would gain the brand as much exposure as possible. The company purchased space in Chinese language newspapers for Chinese holidays as well as traditional American holidays. The full-page print ads appeared in New York and San Francisco.

L³ also designed a special Chinese New Year promotion. The Chinese send red envelopes with lucky money inside for New Year. Remy Martin printed hundreds of thousands of red envelopes, bundled them in packages of 25, and gave them to retailers in Asian communities, who distributed them to consumers.

The advertising agency extended the life of the campaign by creating a special event for Remy Martin to sponsor. Moon Festival banquets were held in the Chinese community, and influential leaders were invited to attend. Of course, Remy Martin cognac was served. Most Americans are unfamiliar with

Courtesy L³ Advertising.

the Moon Festival, but it is an important event in Asian culture. The moon has many connotations to Asians, including serenity, contemplation, and maturity.

The American Management Association applauded L³'s Remy Martin Chinese Moon Festival ad for its sensitivity and elegant design. The ad shows a mixture of Chinese and American cultures. The moon and the Brooklyn Bridge are prominently displayed, indicating a bridge between East and West. In the forefront of the ad are fruits and cake, foods traditionally served during the Moon Festival. A bottle of Remy Martin is the most dramatic visual image in the ad. With only a few images, the ad was able to convey myriad feelings and moods.

Conclusion

The L³ campaign for Remy Martin was successful because of the straightforward approach the agency took to marketing the product. Understanding the Asian consumers' desire for information, L³ designed a campaign that provided them with knowledge about the brand that built on the information they already had.

Another notable aspect of the campaign was its careful usage of Chinese images. The creative team gave readers what they wanted to see, which was a Chinese-language ad that recognized their customs and traditions. The ad also avoided any discussion of Remy Martin's competitors, since Chinese people find it impolite to denounce another product. Without ever mentioning Johnny Walker Red, Remy was able to position its cognac as the prestige brand in the market.

Finally, the campaign was effective because it was neither too subtle nor too heavy-handed. It used a clear concept, expressed through concise language and images to convey a simple message.

DISCUSSION QUESTIONS

1. Should Remy Martin be prepared to face the same criticism leveled against companies that market alcoholic beverages to blacks and Latinos?
2. If so, what should the company's position be?
3. If the brand had not been well established in Asia, what approach should the advertising agency have taken to market it?

Endnotes

1. E. Remy Martin Et Compagnie SA, *Million Dollar Directory: America's Leading Public and Private Companies* (New Jersey: Dun & Bradstreet, 1989).
2. Joshua Levine, ed., "We're at the Wrong End of the Meal," *Forbes* (13 September 1993): 198.
3. Anthony Dias Blue, "The Cognac Mystique," *Bon Appétit* (December 1986): 150.
4. Ibid.
5. Levine, "We're at the Wrong End of the Meal."
6. Ibid.

VIEW FROM THE TOP

Dana Yamagata
Creative Director/Partner
Pacific Rim Advertising

Dana Yamagata is a pioneer of Asian advertising. He has worked with the California Lottery, Vons Supermarkets, Northwest Airlines, Raging Waters, and Pacific Bell Directory. He has produced numerous Asian events with community groups and is actively involved in developing marketing strategies for clients trying to reach Asian consumers.

He previously worked with Young and Rubicam, San Francisco, and Benton Boweles, New York. He is a graduate of San Francisco State University and attended New York University and the School for Visual Arts in New York.

Are the Asian markets very different on the East and West coasts?

Recently arrived Asian immigrants have accounted for the rapid increase in the Asian American population. They have settled or resettled largely by ethnicity in urban areas as well as in suburban pocket areas throughout the United States. There have always been differences among Asians, and there always will be. Regional dialects of Asians differ greatly and can further contribute to communication problems. For example, a Chinese immigrant from Hong Kong who speaks Cantonese may not be able to communicate with a Chinese immigrant from Beijing who speaks the Mandarin dialect. The differences we can associate within the mainstream culture of the West Coast and the East Coast are magnified many times over with the Asian markets.

What is the future of the Asian market?

There is a tremendous future in the Asian market. Immigrant Asians come to the United States for a new life. Asians are characteristically driven to succeed and are supported by a network of family members or relatives. Influenced by peer group pressure, Asians have always been discriminating shoppers conscious of price and good quality.

Is it a mistake to lump the different groups of the Asian market together?

Within the various Asian communities, there is a strong sense of purpose. Individual Asian groups have grown stronger while an effort to build coalitions has been slow to gain support. The lack of English skills contributes to a kind of ethnic isolation.

What is the most important thing for marketers to remember when targeting Asians?

Asians want to be treated with respect. Mainstream marketers who go into the market for the short term often do not take into consideration differences in cultural habits and therefore may embarrass themselves culturally. Over the past few years, marketers have made better attempts to understand the Asian markets and to avoid mistakes made in the past. Too often, these mistakes have cost a marketer its image and perception. Marketers have to take the time and patience to do their homework in Asian markets. These markets are culturally distinct and different in many languages.

Do you have any campaigns that you can discuss that show the difference between the Asian market and mainstream advertising?

The early Asian campaign for the California Lottery took into account what luck meant to the various Asian markets. For instance, the Chinese believe in lucky numbers and good fortune; the Koreans believe in trying their luck if they have a good dream.

What special characteristics have emerged from research on Asian consumers that you have incorporated into an advertising campaign?

Vons Supermarkets in Southern California welcomed Asian shoppers by highlighting quality, freshness, and cleanliness in their television commercials. Vons realized that the Asian shopping priorities are different from the mainstream and tailored their spots to the different Asian markets.

9

Food Store Finds Gold in Hispanic Community

Client: Jewel Food Stores
Agency: Unimar, Inc.
Chicago
Target: Hispanic American families

This case examines merchandising concepts and ideas employed by a major metropolitan grocery to attract business in a changing community. It looks at how one business responded to the different needs and perceptions of a new audience. In addition, it shows how a promotional theme can be completely modified to reach a specific target group.

At the end of this case, students should be able to do the following:

1. Discuss different definitions of "traditional"
2. Understand how merchandisers can take advantage of changing demographics
3. Analyze the influence of culture on message perception

Profile of the Company

Jewel Companies, Inc., is a subsidiary of the American Stores Company, a diversified corporation with net earnings of $199.4 million in 1991.[1] In addition to Jewel Food Stores, American Stores is holder of Lucky Stores, Inc., located in California; American Drug Stores, headquartered in Oak Brook, Illinois; Acme Markets, in Pennsylvania; and Star Markets, in Massachusetts. The Jewel Stores, headquartered in Chicago, employed over 30,000 people in 1992.[2]

Jewel was started by Frank Vernon Skiff in 1899. The tea salesman traveled through Chicago's South Side peddling coffee, spices, house wares, and extracts off his wagon. His first business failed. In 1901, Skiff returned to the grocery business, but this time he was joined by his brother-in-law, Frank Ross. They called the new company Jewel Tea, a name meant to indicate that they were selling items of value. The success of this venture allowed them to open their first store. In 1903, Jewel Tea was incorporated into Jewel Tea Comapny.[3]

The company changed hands by 1920, and by the next year, sales jumped to over $1 million.[4] Jewel later entered the chain-store business and nearly went bankrupt. Research later indicated that Jewel was not providing consumers with what they wanted. The company changed its marketing approach to incorporate the features 18,000 Chicago housewives rated as important.

Over the next few decades, Jewel suffered and prospered with the changing economic conditions of Chicago. Through these times, it held firm to its philosophy that people want and deserve a clean, courteous place to purchase groceries.

By the 1960s, Jewel Stores expanded into Europe, merged with Osco Drugs, and acquired Turn Style Stores. Since that time, a number of acquisitions and purchases have expanded the company's reach and profitability. Jewel was acquired by American Stores in June of 1984.

What Jewel Wanted to Accomplish

Over the years, Jewel's philosophy had not changed; however, the consumers the stores were serving had shifted dramatically. There was a growing and undeniable ethnic audience shopping at Jewel Stores; specifically, the Hispanic population expanded into Chicago's inner city. They were frequent shoppers who spent a sizable portion of their incomes on grocery products.

Jewel established its "Ten Commandments" in 1934: (1) clean and white stores; (2) friendliness; (3) self-service; (4) true quality; (5) freshness; (6) low prices; (7) honest weights; (8) variety of foods; (9) fair dealings; and (10) complete satisfaction or money back with a smile.[5] These principles served the company well with its primary audiences. The question for the company at the end of the 1980s was whether it needed to make adjustments to meet the needs of its new shoppers.

With the help of Unimar Communications research, Jewel Food Stores realized that its approach to the audience indeed needed changing. Grocery shopping is a different experience for Hispanics than for other consumers. Unimar recognized two important facts about Hispanic audiences. First, Hispanic families spend more money per week on groceries than other consumers. This means that Hispanic families are in the grocery store more often than other consumers. Second, Jewel realized that Hispanic consumers are not simply interested in the products a company offers; they also expect that the company will demonstrate its interest and concern for them.

Despite Jewel's long-standing tradition in Chicago neighborhoods, it had little experience dealing with customers of different cultural backgrounds. The foods they eat, how they shop, when they shop, and the expectations they bring to the store all needed to be considered. Jewel wanted customers to feel comfortable in its stores, to visit them often, and to find the products they needed.

Concept/Theme Development

Jewel took the occasion of its 50th anniversary in Chicago to create a campaign aimed at the Hispanic audience. For traditional shoppers, Jewel showed a horse and carriage. It was a nostalgic scene designed to remind shoppers of Jewel's long-standing presence in the community. The store began with one man selling tea and coffee from his wagon.

Because the Hispanic consumer was a relative newcomer to the Chicago scene, the traditional presentation would not be effective. In addition, the Hispanic population is younger than the general audience, so a campaign based on tradition would be meaningless to this group. Recognizing the irrelevance of this campaign to the target audience, Unimar developed a concept with a different twist. Instead of focusing on history, the agency dealt with how Jewel has changed with its customers. It stressed that the store's history was a strong indication that it would be around in the future. The advertising message looked forward, not backward.

The theme "Jewel Is Your Friend" was a simple statement that encompassed all the messages the store wished to communicate. At the same time, it was not a departure from the store's long-time marketing philosophy. The theme also took into consideration the Hispanic community's desire for involvement on the part of the corporation. Shoppers wanted to know that the company cared about them and was willing to demonstrate it openly.

Execution

Unimar created a variety of print ads for the Jewel 50th anniversary campaign. All of the ads centered around the grocery store being a place where consumers could go to find friendly service and the products they needed for their families. The ads showed a lot of food, particularly Hispanic dishes, being prepared and served. Some ads talked about old family recipes, the ingredients for which could be found at Jewel.

Visuals selected for the ads were bright and colorful. The campaign centered around family and the shoppers' desire to satisfy the family with good, fresh food. Jewel's other principles were also included in the ads. The stores were shown as clean places; fair and reasonable pricing was highlighted; and, as always, there was a money-back guarantee. If customers were not satisfied, they could always return the merchandise, and it would be accepted with a smile.

Conclusion

Working with its Hispanic agency, Jewel Food Stores learned that it was not necessary to change the basic marketing principles that had served it well for half a century. However, the company did learn that those philosophies needed to be presented differently to a new and expanding audience.

The campaign was effective because it took into consideration what the target audience viewed as important and used that information as a basis for developing a campaign aimed directly at them. At the same time, the company did not have to alter its basic strategy, since Hispanic consumers have much in common with other members of the shopping population.

Jewel is now the leading grocery store for Hispanic Americans in Chicago. As their numbers increase, it is likely that the store will attract even more Hispanic consumers if it continues to address their needs.

DISCUSSION QUESTIONS ◄-----------------------------

1. In your opinion, what is the single most important aspect of the Jewel campaign?
2. How would you design a general campaign for Jewel not anchored around a special event?
3. Because Hispanic audiences like special attention, what type of in-store promotional campaign would you develop for Jewel Stores?

Endnotes

1. *American Stores Company 1991 Annual Report*, 5.
2. Ibid.
3. American Stores Company, *International Directory of Company Histories*, vol. 1 (Chicago: St. James Press, 1988), 604–606.
4. Ibid.
5. *History of Jewel Companies, Inc.*, Jewel Food Stores, September 1979.

VIEW FROM THE TOP

Marta Miyares ◄-----------------------------
President
Unimar U.S. Hispanic Communications

Marta Miyares, president of Unimar, has been working in the advertising business for 20 years. Unimar U.S. Hispanic Communications is a full-service advertising agency headquartered on Chicago's Magnificent Mile. It offers research, creative services, media, promotions, and public relations to its clients. Unimar has affiliated offices in major U.S. Hispanic markets, including San Antonio, Los Angeles, and Miami.

A native of Cuba, Miyares fled the country when Fidel Castro assumed power. With a degree in architecture, she began as a Montessori teacher and taught at the first bilingual Montessori school in Chicago. She joined Unimar in 1978, filling in as a receptionist at the urging of her husband and the company's founder. He convinced her that she could use her Montessori training to nurture and support employees. She later became manager of client services, and then took over the company in 1981 after her husband purchased a television station.

Miyares is a recipient of the 1987 Hispanic Women in Communications Award, the Illinois Minority Enterprise Development 1988 Advertising and Public Relations Company Award, and the 1990 Business Woman of Achievement Award of the Mexican-American Business and Professional Women. She is a graduate of the 4A's Institute of Advanced Advertising Studies at Northwestern University.

What do clients expect from your agency?

They expect us to be very sensitive to the market. They want us to know what motivates a purchase and to know lifestyles and cultures beyond language. Anybody can translate language from English to Spanish. But an advertisement is more than a mere translation. It is emotions, involvement, impulse.

What do Hispanic consumers want to see in advertising?

We are no different than other consumers. We want to see ourselves on television. The message needs to be relevant to me. Even if I understand the message, it must motivate me to take some action. For example, you might see a party or a bank scenario in an ad. If all of the people look like someone else, if the music is not what we like, if the situations aren't familiar, then the ad won't be convincing. Hispanics are not blond and blue-eyed. The type of interaction we share is different from the mainstream. To be effective, advertising must reflect these differences.

Can you cite an example where a translation of a concept from English to Spanish didn't work?

Sure. In one Ameritech (Illinois Bell) telephone commercial, they showed a little old lady at home alone. The message of the ad was to remind her children to "reach out and call home." The reason this message was ineffective, and maybe even offensive, is because in the Hispanic culture, elders—especially mothers—are cherished. We don't need to be reminded to call our mothers. We would never forget. Also, if our mother or grandmother was home alone, we probably wouldn't call; we'd go visit.

People, maybe even some clients, tend to lump minority groups together. What distinguishes the two largest groups, African Americans and Hispanics, from one another?

It is a mistake to ignore the differences that exist between African Americans and Hispanic consumers. Hispanics share some characteristics with African Americans. For example, there is a Caribbean connection and a love of music. But because of their longer history in this country, African Americans have different aspirations than Hispanics. Most of us are still in the stage of trying to have a roof over our heads, decent clothing, and education. African Americans are farther down the road in terms of political and economic clout. This means the two groups will respond differently to advertising appeals. You can market a Cadillac to black audiences, but it's too big a jump to show a Cadillac to the majority of the Hispanic market. Not many Hispanic people can afford a Cadillac.

What does appeal to Hispanic audiences?

You have to understand some things about the Hispanic market. A family appeal is very important. Religion and traditional values are also important to the Hispanic audience. Hispanic people like things that are beautiful as well. Hispanic women like to dress up—even to go to the grocery store. We like to dress up our little girls too. We take pride and pleasure in looking good. Some might mistake this for showing off, but it's not. We are just doing what comes naturally.

How does Hispanic culture influence advertising concepts you develop?

It's no secret that Hispanic people like movement, visuals, and bright colors. We come from countries where the sun shines. I think the light affects our sense of color. We have a well-defined sense of contrast. Our executions should always include color. We show people who are more expressive with their hands, people who tend to be louder, lots of flowers and makeup. Our commercials should always contain music, if it's appropriate.

How does being an immigrant affect the consumer behavior of Hispanics?

Once Hispanic people come to the United States, most change. Many still speak Spanish at home, where the advertising message is most likely to reach them. Where they came from, their mothers sometimes had to work in factories to help the family survive. When you arrive in this country, you are influenced by the neighborhood, the dominant culture, and the media. The Hispanic culture is traditionally male dominated. In this country, women work, take care of a home, and make major purchasing decisions. An advertising agency must take the traditional and the new into consideration when creating ads for this market.

We hear a lot of discussion about the differences within the Spanish market. For example, there are Puerto Ricans, Cubans, Mexicans, and Central Americans. How do these differences affect the advertising message?

Yes, all Hispanic groups are different. But, it's not so much a matter of where you come from as where you live now. New York is heavily concentrated with Puerto Ricans; Miami has a high concentration of Cubans. If you live in one of these locations, you are likely to be influenced by the particular Hispanic culture that is dominant there.

In what ways do clients tend to misunderstand the marketplace?

Unfortunately, there are still prejudices and stereotypes. Most advertising clients don't live in the market. They don't know Hispanics. I don't blame them. They simply don't know who we are; they're not familiar with the way we look, talk, or eat. Most Mexicans get their first taco when they come to America. Mexicans don't eat tacos in Mexico. We (the agency) must educate the clients and earn their trust.

The Big Brew Ha Ha over Malt Liquor

Client: G. Heileman Brewing
PowerMaster/Crazy Horse

Target: African Americans
Hispanic Americans
Native Americans

This case discusses the problems associated with marketing a product in the midst of uncontrollable social and ethical controversy. G. Heileman Brewing Company faced several problems in its efforts to market PowerMaster and Crazy Horse. First, it ran into trouble with the government over the name "PowerMaster," and Native Americans protested the name "Crazy Horse." Second, the Surgeon General and the Secretary of Health and Human Services criticized the products because they targeted minority consumers who may be more susceptible to increased health risks associated with alcohol use. Third, a Catholic priest led the fight against the product. His involvement further complicated the problem by adding moral and religious concerns to the issue.

At the end of this case students should be able to discuss the following:

1. The moral implications of marketing specific products to ethnic audiences
2. How a product name can stir emotional responses in ethnic audiences
3. The problems alcohol manufacturers face in marketing their popular problems in an antidrug social climate

4. When marketers should make a decision against marketing a product despite possibilities for major financial gains
5. Who should decide what is sold to whom
6. The options a manufacturer has when trying to penetrate ethnic markets

Profile of the Company

According to Dun and Bradstreet, G. Heileman Brewing Company was America's fastest-growing brewer of premium beer in 1987.[1] Located in LaCross, Wisconsin, Heileman produces 34 different brands of malt liquor, low-calorie beer, and near beer. Some of its best-sellers are Old Style, Pilsner, and Special Export. The company operates a sophisticated and widespread distribution system that helps it supply its products throughout the country.[2]

Heileman was founded in 1853 by a German immigrant with an American partner. The company was incorporated in 1918.

Old Style Beer, the brew for which the company is best known, was copyrighted in 1902.

The company survived Prohibition, took a downturn during World War II, and sustained rapid growth in the 1960s and 1970s, when it acquired 13 regional breweries. In the decade between 1956 and 1966, Heileman's profits doubled from $15 million to $31.9 million.[3]

Despite its growth, Heileman was ranked only 22nd in the beer industry in 1967. A year later it moved to 18th.[4] By 1973, Heileman found itself engaged in an antitrust battle as a result of the purchase of three breweries from the Associated Brewing Company. It was ruled that Heileman could keep its acquisitions if it divested itself of several brands. The Justice Department also ruled that Heileman could not purchase any breweries in the Midwest for 10 years.

Stroh and Schmidt breweries filed another antitrust suit against Heileman in 1983. The companies contended that the merger would create a monopoly for beer sales in the Midwest. The courts ruled in favor of Heileman, so the company's growth continued. It expanded its reach to other regions with the purchase of the Lone Star Brewing Company in 1984.

From its inception, Heileman has been viewed as a regional, rather than national, brewery. The company is now competing for a larger share of the national market through its expansion into different regions such as the Southwest and the Southeast.

➤ What G. Heileman Wanted to Accomplish

Like all beer manufacturers, Heileman wanted to grab a larger share of the growing beer market. To do so, it would need to expand its reach to new consumers. African Americans, Hispanics, and Native Americans were already users of Heileman's products, so the company decided to take advantage of its toehold on these markets by increasing promotion aimed at these targets.

To reach African Americans, Heileman developed PowerMaster, a potent malt liquor marketed under the Colt 45 brand name. Heileman called the brew "the answer to those consumers who desire an up-strength product." It was developed to compete against Olde English 800, Schlitz Red Bull, and St. Ides, all of which contained a high alcohol content. But PowerMaster's alcohol content was 5.9 percent, as compared with other malt liquors ranging from 4.5 percent to 5.4 percent. Traditional beer has an alcohol content of 3.5 percent.

In the case of Crazy Horse, a product manufactured by G. Heileman but marketed by Hornell Brewing Company of Brooklyn, New York, Hornell said it was not trying to reach the Native American population. It claimed it was marketing Crazy Horse as one in a series of malts named for western legends, like Annie Oakley Lite and Jim Bowie Pilsner. The makers of Crazy Horse ran into problems in a previous attempt to market the product. The Bureau of Alcohol Tobacco and Firearms (BATF) found the brand's labeling misleading. The marketers removed phrases from the label like "fine blend" and "registered at the brewery," because the agency said they gave the impression that the brand was a whiskey and not a malt liquor.

➤ Concept/Theme Development

PowerMaster's name was indicative of how it would be positioned to the target audience. The name implied that the drink was powerful and that those who drank it were in control. Because of the high alcohol content of the malt, Lockhart and Pettus developed the theme "Bold, Not Harsh" to describe the taste of the product. The theme was a departure from Colt 45's image as a drink that aided sexual prowess. The brand had used celebrities, like actor Billy Dee Williams and retired football player Fred "the Hammer" Williamson, to promote the drink. There were a number of ads featuring women in sexy poses, under silk sheets, waiting for men who drank Colt 45. For PowerMaster, the focus was to be on taste, rather than overt sexuality.

In the case of Crazy Horse the name also served as a positioning tool. The use of the Indian Chief's name was a double entendre. It allowed the company to take advantage of name recognition, while implying that the drink would make one go crazy.

Outcomes

Both brews met with fierce opposition. The BATF ordered the makers of PowerMaster to stop distributing promotional material because it was in violation of the Federal Alcohol Administration Act, which prohibits alcohol marketers from using obscenity, indecency, or disparagement of a competitor to promote products. In addition, alcohol advertising cannot mislead the public or make therapeutic claims. Heileman denied that it was promoting the brand on the basis of alcohol content.

Twenty-one consumer and health groups called for the marketing of the product to be stopped. Before PowerMaster was released, two Catholic priests organized a movement to stop it. PowerMaster was pulled before it was released. The Bureau of Alcohol Tobacco and Firearms, which had originally given PowerMaster the green light, reversed its original position and repealed its approval of the brand. The BATF reviewed other brands and ordered breweries to "cease this type of advertising."

Colt 45 returned in 1993 with an ad campaign in which a clean-cut black male in a shirt and tie is shown relaxing on his front porch in what appears to be an inner-city neighborhood. "I was the first in my family to go to college. It was a night school thing, which is cool, because now I can do some things good." This ad was criticized by the *New York Times* and others who viewed it as just another way of glamorizing malt liquor.

In 1991, *Advertising Age* named PowerMaster "Product of the Year." It was the first never-released product to earn the distinction.

On the other hand, Crazy Horse was distributed but not without resistance. Surgeon General Antonia Novello went to a Sioux Indian reservation and asked the leaders to help her fight the brand. She harshly criticized Hornell for what she called "insensitive and malicious marketing." She noted the high incidence of alcohol abuse among Native Americans and called for a campaign to stop this "exploitation."

A number of lawmakers followed suit. The House passed a bill banning the BATF from approving additional Crazy Horse labels; the Senate Appropriations Committee ordered Hornell to negotiate with the Oglala Sioux Indian tribe about possibly changing the name. The talks broke down without resolution. The Senate later removed Hornell's federal license to sell Crazy Horse, giving the marketer one day to sell bottles already on the shelf.

The controversy and publicity surrounding the marketing of Crazy Horse actually boosted the brand in a number of markets. Bottles were illegally smuggled into some locations where the brand was not available, sending the price soaring. Critics of the alcohol industry waged a media battle against defenders of the First Amendment. A *Wall Street Journal* writer denounced the legislation against Hornell, calling it "The Second Murder of Crazy Horse."[5]

Hornell fought the legislation against its brand and eventually won the right to market Crazy Horse. A federal judge in Brooklyn found that the congressional law to prohibit the use of the name "Crazy Horse" was unconstitutional and an infringement of the First Amendment rights of Hornell. The judge cited examples of other brews that use the names of Native American symbols and leaders, such as Thunderbird wine, Sitting Bull, and Chief Osh Kosh Red Lager. The ruling did not satisfy many Native Americans, but it was a victory for the brewers and marketers.

A Sioux tribal judge said naming a malt liquor after Crazy Horse was tantamount to naming a police baton after Rodney King.

DISCUSSION QUESTIONS ◄-------------------------------

1. Should companies manufacturing and marketing products of a sensitive nature float "trial balloons" in the media before launching their products?
2. Should government regulate the sale of particular products to ethnic groups?
3. What is the role of the public relations department of a company involved in marketing unpopular products?
4. How would you change the name and the theme of PowerMaster's advertising and develop a new campaign?
5. Does/should the First Amendment protect advertisers from any form of governmental regulation, no matter what the product?

Endnotes

1. G. Heileman Brewing Company, Inc., *International Directory of Company Histories,* vol. 1 (Chicago: St. James Press, 1988), 253–255.
2. Ibid., 253.
3. Ibid., 254.
4. Ibid.
5. James Bovard, "The Second Murder of Crazy Horse," *Wall Street Journal* (15 September 1992).

VIEW FROM THE TOP

Vince Cullers
President/Chief Executive Officer
Cullers Advertising

Ethnic advertising as we know it today began with Vince Cullers, often referred to as the dean of black advertising. He founded the nation's first black-owned, full-service agency in 1956.

A native of Chicago, Cullers graduated from DuSable High School. His interest in art prompted him to attend the Chicago Art Institute. In addition, Cullers studied business at the University of Chicago. He later worked as a marketing consultant to a number of white agencies.

Cullers's advertising career began in 1953 at *Ebony* magazine, where he served as art director. Although he was approached by mainstream agencies, Cullers decided to start his own business. Working with his wife, Marian Cullers, he opened Cullers Advertising, Inc., as a way for businesses to reach the growing African American population.

He is involved with a number of community organizations, including Operation PUSH, the Chicago Advertising Club, the NAACP, the Cosmopolitan Chamber of Commerce, the Urban League, and the Assault on Illiteracy Program.

In the more than 30 years since he began in the industry, Cullers Advertising has represented companies like Johnson Products, Amoco, Kellogg, Pizza Hut, and Sears. In addition, his agency has won a number of CEBA awards.

How has ethnic advertising changed over the past three decades?

Thirty years ago, we were the one and only ethnic agency. We were inventing the wheel. The market potential was tremendous even then. The black consumer was not very difficult to reach. There were strong, clear definitions of what black people were. Today, black people have evolved. The emerging market is still black, but many of us are still trying to assimilate. This makes it more difficult to penetrate and reach the black audience.

What hasn't changed?

The ethnic agencies still seldom have the budgets the general market agencies receive—but that doesn't mean we produce ads of lower quality. In fact, we are forced to be more innovative because we have less to work with. In the final analysis, it's not money that produces excellent advertising for clients— it's talent. Clients respect talent.

Was it difficult for you in the beginning?

Yes, but it's always hard to start something new and different. The general condition for blacks in the business was bad. I'm sorry to say it's not too much better now. There was and is a problem of racism. When we began, white clients were reluctant to spend money on the black market. They didn't understand it. Some didn't even believe it existed. We spent a lot of frustrating years knowing we had the knowledge to get a job done that others didn't even realize needed to be done.

When did major clients begin to understand specialized marketing?

I would say that it was during the 1960s. Astute businesses recognized a change that was taking place in the black community. They could see the need for special marketing programs aimed at black communities. They started to see that "there was gold in them there hills."

Tell me about one of your more memorable campaigns.

The Afro Sheen ads of the late 1960s stand out as a classic. In the ads, we were able to portray pride, family, and heritage at a time when black people were beginning to recognize who they were. Black people found a positive self-image during this period. Campaigns like Afro Sheen crystallized that image and provided black people with a reflection of themselves.

Is it better for young people to begin at a small agency or a large one?

Young people should get involved—wherever it is. Some don't want to work with black agencies. Some want to join major advertising firms. We also need entrepreneurs and people who will make contributions to the community. For years, own agency actually functioned as a training ground for many young blacks seeking their first exposure to the ad industry. We would teach them and they would move on. It was not the best way to develop a business, but I enjoyed it.

Your agency began during a time prior to affirmative action. How did you get clients?

I admit that some of our clients came as a result of pressure placed on white companies to do business with the black community. Operation Breadbasket (now Operation PUSH) and the NAACP were instrumental in getting companies to understand that they needed to support black businesses. My first client, Lorillard of New York, came that way. Acquiring that account opened the door to other accounts for us.

If you could begin your career again, would you be an ad man?

Absolutely! This is one of the most exciting, rewarding careers in the world. Despite the hardships, I would do it all over again.

Tarzan Trades in Trees for Toyota Truck

Client:	Toyota
Agency:	Conill Advertising
	New York
Target Audience:	Hispanic males

This final case looks at how a popular mainstream character is used to market a product to an ethnic audience. The use of humor is also explored in this case.

The international and multicultural perspective of this case is particularly interesting. Conill Advertising took a product made in Japan and developed a campaign for it featuring a European character who just happened to live in Africa; then it targeted that campaign to a Hispanic audience.

To be successful, the commercial would need to overcome biases, take into account cultural differences and preferences, and take advantage of the Hispanic market's love for humor in advertising.

At the end of this chapter, you should be able to do the following:

1. Understand how ethnic advertising can effectively use nonethnic characters
2. Discuss some of the commonalities between ethnic and nonethnic advertising
3. Recognize the difference between a negative stereotype and an honest characterization

➤ Profile of the Company

Toyota was the first Japanese automaker's name Americans came to know. The first Toyota vehicle was produced in 1935. At that time the company was known as Toyoda, named for its founder, Kiichiro Toyoda. World War II severely damaged Toyota's operations, but the company was rebuilt after the war ended. Realizing that it would be difficult to compete with General Motors and the other U.S. car manufacturers in the large auto market, Toyota made a conscious decision to focus its efforts on manufacturing smaller autos.

During the late 1940s, Toyota enjoyed success and confronted failure in its effort to become a major player in worldwide auto sales. There were labor disputes, an economic depression, missed marketing opportunities, and overall flat sales.

The 1950s brought foreign competition to the Japanese car market. Both U.S. and European automakers began to sell cars to Japanese consumers. The company responded by lowering production costs, developing better cars, and strengthening quality. By 1966, the Toyota Corolla was Japan's most popular family car.

The oil crisis of 1973 helped Toyota and other small car manufacturers penetrate the U.S. market. As fuel prices rose, so did Americans' dissatisfaction with gas-guzzling cars. Toyota was well positioned to market its cars to American consumers. Toyota's cars were smaller, more fuel efficient, and cheaper than their U.S. counterparts.

There would later be an American backlash against Japanese automobiles as U.S. manufacturing jobs were lost. Based on its knowledge and understanding of American car buyers, Toyota decided to aggressively pursue proactive public relations strategies aimed at the bitter American audience. The company would acknowledge its position of leadership, push a dialogue about the value of free trade, and build a Toyota plant in America, employing American workers.

By the end of 1992, U.S. Toyota sales were nearly $16 billion.[1]

➤ What Toyota Wanted to Accomplish

Simply stated, Toyota wanted to sell more cars than its major competitors. Not only did the company face stiff competition from U.S. automakers, it had to confront challenges from other Asian carmakers as well. The Honda Accord was the best-selling car in America for four straight years. Nissan had a sizable share of the market; Mazda made substantial inroads into the U.S. market; and Isuzu and Hyundai—the newer kids on the block—were quickly gaining acceptance.

With such heavy saturation and so many choices for the American driver who wanted a foreign car, Toyota sought to expand its market by pursuing nontraditional consumers. African Americans were more likely to purchase foreign cars from Europe, such as Mercedes Benz and BMW. The Asian American market, though a good potential audience, was too small to make a major contribution to Toyota's overall sales. Hispanic drivers, on the other hand, were an ideal audience for Toyota products. First, Hispanics enjoy cars (73 percent of all U.S. Hispanics own at least one automobile).[2] Research also indicated that auto ownership for Hispanics was heaviest in the Northeast, and multiple car ownership was highest in the Southwest.[3] Lifestyle considerations of residents of Southwestern states indicated the utility of owning a truck as either a first or second vehicle.

Concept/Theme Development

Conill Advertising positioned the Toyota truck as the vehicle of choice for smart Hispanics. The truck was also aimed directly at male drivers, who are most likely to make car-purchasing decisions in Hispanic families. The concept addressed several consumer traits attributed to Hispanic audiences. The campaign focused on humor and tradition—both identified as characteristics important in reaching the target group. The sight of an aging Tarzan was unusual enough and unique enough to grab the attention of the audience. Tarzan's popularity with Hispanic audiences was also used in developing this campaign. The legendary hero was easily recognizable and carried with him a host of mythological images. Because of the familiarity of the Tarzan character, the ad itself did not need to waste time identifying him or explaining his role.

Conill also designed the ad to demonstrate and poke fun at what Carlos Rossi called the "chauvinism" that often exists in Hispanic cultures. Tarzan's work is obviously "man's work." He lives with animals, wrestles with them, and is usually victorious over jungle beasts. Tarzan also has a reputation for controlling his woman as well as his environment. After all, a prim and proper British lady relinquished all her worldly possessions to join him in the jungle. In other words, Tarzan is a man's man.

Execution

Conill used television to exhibit the ruggedness and utility of Toyota trucks. The ad they developed featured an obviously Hispanic Tarzan, dressed in his familiar loincloth, looking particularly tired and mature. The jungle hero has lots of ground to cover but is not making the best use of his time or energy by flying around in trees. It occurs to Tarzan that his efforts would be better served if he purchased a pickup truck.

With the help of the truck, Tarzan was able to go from one jungle location to the next with relative ease. The versatility of the truck allowed Tarzan to perform a variety of activities while sustaining less wear and tear on his slightly out-of-shape body.

Television allowed for graphic visuals. It would be more difficult to convey the image of an aging Tarzan through other media. The jungle setting, the distinctive yell, the tree swinging—all associated with the character—were easily demonstrated in the commercial.

There were several humorous elements in the ad. First, an aging Tarzan attempted to maintain his machismo, despite the fact that age had caught up with him. His decision to purchase a Toyota truck was the next best thing to swinging on vines. Visuals and copy work together in this ad to make the viewer pay attention, laugh, empathize, and, it is hoped, act.

Conclusion

The Toyota Tarzan case demonstrates that many of the same appeals used to advertise to the general market can be effective in reaching ethnic audiences. However, it is important to note that the image selected was one that was already popular with the target group. The ad might not have been as successful if the character chosen was, for example, Robin Hood. Like Tarzan, Robin Hood is legendary and romantic. But the major difference between the two is where each one operated. Tarzan lived in a tropical, colorful climate—one to which the audience could relate.

This case, like all others in the text, demonstrates the importance of conducting meaningful research and appropriately applying the results. The

TOYOTA 4X4 TRUCK   HISPANIC

"TRUCKZAN"

LENGTH : 30

TRUCKZAN: Desde que compré mi camioneta Toyota 4X4,
TRUCKZAN: Since I bought my Toyota 4X4 truck,

ya no ando de árbol en árbol.
no more going from tree to tree.

Con mi Toyota,
With my Toyota,

voy por cualquier camino.
I go on any road.

Toyota 4X4 tiene
Toyota 4X4 has

potente motor V6.
powerful V6 engine.

Y cuando voy a pasear por ciudad,
And when I go to the city,

poderosa Toyota
mighty Toyota

me hace lucir bien.
makes me look good.

Porque una cosa es Chita,
Because one thing is Cheetah.

y otra, muchachita.
and another is mucha-"cheetah" (girl).

SINGERS: Estás hecho para mí, Toyota.
SINGERS: You were made for me, Toyota.

To order dealer version, call
(213) 938-2872 and ask for
Commercial TC-91-25/05TV#100

"Estás hecho para mí."

TOYOTA

® 1991 TOYOTA MOTOR SALES, U.S.A. INC.

Courtesy Conill Advertising.

important data to emerge from Hispanic audience research for this case were the preponderance of auto purchases by male Hispanics and the effectiveness of humor in developing and executing ads for this market. Conill took full advantage of these facts and blended them together into a memorable campaign for Toyota trucks.

Conill might have been criticized for simply "colorizing" a Caucasian character. One of the problems ethnic audiences have with mainstream advertising is that it sometimes takes white characters and "paints" them a different color with little regard to cultural behavior, preferences, or lifestyles. However, in this case, what might appear as a colorization on the surface was really substantially more. The Toyota Tarzan was behaving like a Hispanic male. He was smart and assertive, and he found he liked to drive.

The campaign could have taken a wrong turn by using a "gang-banging" Hispanic male, living in East Los Angeles, who used his Toyota truck to make lots of noise in the "hood" (translation, neighborhood). Doing so would have stereotyped the Hispanic male. And although it is true that a small number of Hispanic men do belong to gangs, that segment is not representative of the entire group, and thus does not give an accurate portrayal of the population.

DISCUSSION QUESTIONS ◄---------------------------------

1. Would the same campaign be transferable to African American audiences? If so, how? If not, why not?
2. Is there any way to modify this campaign so that it would not be possibly offensive to Hispanic women?
3. What different strategy might the advertising agency have used to reach the target audience?

Endnotes

1. "Toyota," *Standard and Poors Register of Corporations, Directors and Executives,* vol. 1 (New York: McGraw-Hill, 1993), 2639.
2. *1987 Hispanic Market Study* (Miami: Strategy Research Corporation, 1987), 558.
3. Ibid., 531.

VIEW FROM THE TOP

Byron Lewis
President/Chief Executive Officer
UniWorld

Byron Lewis, known in the advertising business as a master marketer, has lived on the East Coast all of his life. He attended Long Island University, where he studied journalism and earned a bachelor of arts degree in public relations. Because in the 1950s, there were few, if any, jobs in corporate advertising and public relations for an African American male, he went to work for a black newspaper in Harlem as an editorial and publishing assistant. He later found a weekend job with the *New York Times*, working in the classified advertising department. He saw the want ads before they were printed, and he used this advantage to apply for jobs in his field. His qualifications gained him interviews, but he was often denied positions. He began his own advertising agency in 1969.

More than 30 years later, UniWorld's client roster includes AT&T, Burger King, Coors Brewing Company, Eastman Kodak, Lincoln Mercury, Motown, Quaker Oats (Gatorade), and Reebok International, Ltd. The agency also operates a Hispanic division and an entertainment division.

Your communications career spans 30 years. How have you lasted so long?

I've been both a generalist and an "idea" person. I've been open to new and exciting ideas. I believe in being around people with imagination—people who ask "what if?" That helps keep the business exciting. I managed to stay in the business because I was persistent and maybe somewhat naive. I kept answering job advertisements when I had the qualifications for the job. I thought if I could do the job, I should get the job. I never let the fact that I was black bother me, even when it bothered others.

Why did you start your own agency?

I had no other options. I was unable to work in a major mainstream agency, and the clients I met selling black media encouraged me.

What special qualities do your employees have?

All of our minority professionals come from mainstream Madison Avenue agencies. People here have a wide range of interests. They know how to present. They know how to write, and they understand the client/agency relationship. UniWorld people understand the concept of service. In addition, our people are rooted in the fundamentals. They are smart people with solid financial and management skills.

You have created the UniWorld Uniplan. What is it?

Uniplan is our business philosophy. We provide a wide spectrum of targeted, in-house advertising, special events, direct response, and public relations services. In addition, we offer syndicated television production services. What we are doing with Uniplan is assuring maximum ethnic penetration. We're getting direct community contact, good publicity, and word-of-mouth association.

Your agency has a Hispanic division. Was it an afterthought?

We are very proud of our Hispanic operation. We expanded into this area as our business dictated that we needed to. Hispanic markets were not an afterthought for UniWorld. These markets have enjoyed explosive growth in the past few years. The expertise we had in ethnic marketing was transferable to the Hispanic marketplace. The people who work in our Hispanic division are just as talented and knowledgeable as those who work in our other areas.

Your agency is also in the entertainment business. How does that work?

All minorities, African Americans in particular, have been damaged by the lack of visibility or no positive imagery in the media. The same skills we use to create advertising and public relations can be used in promoting more positive cultural images. Take the movie *Glory*, for example. We worked with Kodak to create educational historical study guides for students. They learned about the contributions of blacks during the Civil War and were entertained at the same time.

What type of television work do you do?

Television that is informative and educational. "America's Black Forum" is a one-of-a-kind program bringing news and information about black issues around the world. We do the "Black Filmmaker's Hall of Fame," an annual television special featuring the work of talented black artists. Everything we do has some relevance to the community.

What changes have you seen in advertising in your three decades in the business?

There have been many. It is refreshing to hear black music in advertising. The business covenants created by the Reverend Jesse Jackson and others helped businesses establish relationships with the black community. There are the contributions of a publication like *Ebony*, which helped create a popular understanding of the black market. There is a greater ethnic presence in advertising. There are more sophisticated black communities. I take personal pleasure in seeing these positive changes.

From the Hispanic perspective, there is a growing respect for Hispanic audiences. They have buying power, sophistication, and size. That combination makes them a group to be dealt with. All of our ads take into consideration how the Hispanic population in this country lives, what they think about, and what they want.

That sounds good, but what about negative imagery that still exists?

We still need to improve the portrayal of ethnic people in advertising. Most commercials that use black and Hispanic people are done by white agencies. They will use black talent like Michael Jordan, Gloria Estefan, Ray Charles, Bill Cosby, and Magic Johnson. But they are used to reach everyone, not just black people or Hispanic people. Talent loses color at the superstar level. So, in many cases, there is no sincere interest in reaching black consumers, and black agencies don't have the money or the clout to compete.

Does a minority advertising agency have a greater responsibility than any other agency to be socially conscious?

I evaluate and carefully examine a product before we decide to take on a client. I would not want this agency to contribute to the social and economic ills already facing our communities. I think any agency should act responsibly.

Conclusion

This final chapter focuses on what can be learned from the cases presented. It reviews salient points, discusses the basic principles from the winning strategies, and gives one last postmortem on the unsuccessful campaigns. The future of marketing and advertising to minority consumers is explored, and the trends, fads, changes in regulation, and changes in social behavior that might have an impact on the advertising industry as it relates to ethnic audiences are also discussed.

After finishing this chapter, students should have gained knowledge of the following:

1. The dos and don'ts of ethnic marketing
2. What the future holds for marketing and advertising
3. How basic and advanced marketing techniques provide the fundamentals for advertising to ethnic audiences

What It All Means

The cases presented in this text are in no way a comprehensive representation of marketing and advertising to minority audiences. They are samples of how agencies and companies are approaching this diverse group of consumers.

From each case, there is something to be learned about marketing in general and about marketing to ethnic audiences specifically. Perhaps the most important lessons illustrated by the cases are that no two situations are exactly the same, that no two ethnic minority groups behave the same, and that new data and situations will require different and appropriate techniques.

Following is a review of the major conclusions that can be drawn from each case.

Stove Top Stuffing

Advertising/Marketing Lessons

An old product can be rejuvenated by attracting ethnic consumers.
Familiar images spark interest in ethnic consumers.
Advertising can help extend usage of seasonal products.
Ethnic audiences perceive products differently than the general population does.

General Motors

Advertising/Marketing Lessons

Institutional advertising can be effective in reaching ethnic audiences.
Ethnic audiences are concerned that companies respect their consumer power.
Ethnic consumers respond to spokespersons with high credibility.

Scott Paper Company

Advertising/Marketing Lessons

Hispanic Americans like advertising that uses their native language.
An unexciting product can gain acceptance with an effective advertising campaign.
Issues of family and tradition are important values that can be used in advertising to Hispanic audiences.
Color and animation can be effective tools in creating ads for Hispanic audiences.

Metropolitan Life

Advertising/Marketing Lessons

Immigrants have special concerns and needs that advertisers must address.
Asian American consumers bring cultural mores and taboos to their perceptions of advertising messages.
Asian Americans can be reached by messages that center on family and children.

Uptown Cigarettes

Advertising/Marketing Lessons

Niche marketing can be controversial when dealing with ethnic audiences.
More sophisticated ethnic audiences are likely to reject certain products.
Marketing and advertising campaigns can be tried and judged in the media.
Manufacturers may need to find a way to kick their own habit of marketing unpopular products to ethnic audiences.

United Negro College Fund

Advertising/Marketing Lessons

It is possible to market an ethnic product to a nonethnic audience without backlash.

Advertising messages evolve to match the mood of the receiving audience.
Effective advertising always creates in the consumer an urge to act.
Classic advertising stands up to the test of time.

American Honda

Advertising/Marketing Lessons

An all-American theme can help create the image of an all-American company.
It is possible to counteract negative perceptions by creating messages aimed
distinctly at the target audience.
A special event can serve as the cornerstone for an entire advertising and public
relations campaign.
Targeted media can be used effectively to create awareness of the campaign
with ethnic audiences.

Remy Martin

Advertising/Marketing Lessons

Advertisers need to have an understanding of cultural traditions.
Marketers must be sensitive to nuances of language, visuals, and customs.
Advertising can acculturate first-generation immigrants and still respect the
values of their cultural heritage.
High price can be used as a positioning tool when developing a campaign for
specific ethnic audiences.

Jewel Food Stores

Advertising/Marketing Lessons

It is important to maintain a clear channel of communication from consumers
to retailers.
Campaigns need to appeal to specific cultural traditions.
Ethnic audiences want to see community involvement.

PowerMaster/Crazy Horse

Advertising/Marketing Lessons

Use of negative stereotypical images can backfire when marketing to ethnic audiences.
Marketing products that could be detrimental to health carry specific risks for the advertiser.
Marketers must be sensitive to the cultural and social climate.
Products can be marketed effectively, but advertisers need to rethink images with which they associate the products.

Toyota Trucks

Advertising/Marketing Lessons

Mainstream characters can be used to market ethnic products if cultural differences are considered.
Humor is an effective tool in reaching Hispanic audiences.
There is no substitution for good research before developing an advertising strategy and subsequent campaign.

There are numerous other examples of effective and failed marketing efforts aimed at ethnic audiences. With each of them, there is a lesson for advertisers to consider.

Among the successful cases is Hallmark Cards of Kansas City, Missouri, which launched a specialized greeting card line for Hispanic and African American consumers. Primor cards, which were created for Hispanic audiences, are Spanish-language cards. The Mahagony line, designed for African Americans, features distinctly black images and messages.

In 1993, Spiegel, a 150-year-old Chicago-based catalog company, joined forces with *Ebony* magazine to create a new catalog aimed directly at minority women. This venture, which was the first of its kind, involved narrow target marketing. The catalog, *E-Style,* features clothing designed specifically for African American women. Bold styles and colors and moderate pricing are the characteristics that distinguish the catalog from others. It is targeted to over 1 million African American women, who are either readers of *Ebony* or Spiegel customers.

The Ameritech Company developed a series of advertising messages aimed at Hispanic audiences. In addition to urging Hispanic consumers to use the telephone more often, they hired over 50 bilingual operators to help the customers use the phone more easily.

Other companies have not fared as well. *Reader's Digest International* attempted to reach the Chinese audience with an ad that read, "One thousand things to see in China." Unfortunately, they changed one character, creating an indistinguishable message about planting. *Playboy* magazine forgot that Chinese people read from right to left in its full-page ad in the New *York Times.* One misplaced character created an ad reading, "Year New Happy."

Often marketers are reluctant to deal with ethnic audiences for fear of making mistakes like the ones listed above. It is difficult for them to understand what will be offensive and what messages are acceptable. For them, it is easier to pick up ethnic consumers who are exposed to mainstream messages.

But as media become more segmented and audiences become more diverse, it will be harder to reach ethnic consumers through general market campaigns. And, as these audiences begin to understand their strength as consumers, they will be able to make choices about with whom they do business and where and how they spend their money.

➤ A Look Toward the Future

Today's advertising students will enter an industry much different from the one in which their predecessors worked. "The Man in the Gray Flannel Suit" is being replaced by the woman in the Liz Claiborne dress or the ethnic professional, whose suit may be of any color.

Madison Avenue now shares the advertising spotlight with Chicago's Michigan Avenue and Los Angeles's Wilshire Boulevard. Consumers come in all shapes and sizes. Some speak English; many don't. The marketplace has expanded to include the countries of the Eastern Bloc, South America, and the ever-growing Pacific Basin.

Trends, clothing, and behaviors once considered to be ethnic have spread to the mainstream culture. There are young Caucasians who dress black, talk black, and act black. When developing an advertising campaign for teenage clothing, a marketer might want to consider this cross-cultural phenomenon. Even in Japan, African American culture is what's happening. International advertisers, too, will need to examine the behavior of audiences carefully before designing messages to reach them.

Some of these fads are surely fleeting. Today's white teen who calls himself a "wigger" (a term created from the words *white* and *nigger*) may become tomorrow's businessman. But as trends come and go, there are likely to be some constants. The marketplace will continue to evolve faster and more dramatically than ever before.

Advertising students who are trained strictly in the ways of single-culture communication will find themselves at a distinct disadvantage. They may be able to write, but will they know what to say? They may understand media planning, but will they know who reads what?

It may be time for advertising students to reorder H. Laswell's famous communication question, "Who says what to whom in what channel with what effect?" The question for marketers in today's environment is, "To whom is what said, in what channel with what effect?" Advertisers must know to whom they are speaking before they can design the message, purchase the media time, and measure the results.

In other words, advertising will have to change if it is to remain the powerful and pervasive economic force it has traditionally been in American culture. The industry must recognize the ethnocentric perspective of different audiences and market directly to these distinctions. The advertising business must take a page from its own book if it is to survive the turbulent and dramatic demographic changes that are occurring. It is a business standing on the brink of decline unless it is willing to repackage, redesign, and remarket itself as a "new and improved" entity capable and willing to tackle tomorrow's consumers.

DISCUSSION QUESTIONS ◄-------------------------------

1. What do the cases tell us about the current and future marketplace?
2. What are the principles that held constant throughout all the cases?
3. What distinctions need to be made about ethnic consumers?

I N D E X